FEB 24 2021

I0360598

HBR Guide to
Remote
Work

Harvard Business Review Guides

Arm yourself with the advice you need to succeed on the job, from the most trusted brand in business. Packed with how-to essentials from leading experts, the HBR Guides provide smart answers to your most pressing work challenges.

The titles include:

HBR Guide for Women at Work

HBR Guide to Being More Productive

HBR Guide to Better Business Writing

HBR Guide to Building Your Business Case

HBR Guide to Buying a Small Business

HBR Guide to Changing Your Career

HBR Guide to Coaching Employees

HBR Guide to Data Analytics Basics for Managers

HBR Guide to Dealing with Conflict

HBR Guide to Delivering Effective Feedback

HBR Guide to Emotional Intelligence

HBR Guide to Finance Basics for Managers

HBR Guide to Getting the Mentoring You Need

HBR Guide to Getting the Right Job

HBR Guide to Getting the Right Work Done

HBR Guide to Leading Teams

HBR Guide to Making Better Decisions

HBR Guide to Making Every Meeting Matter

HBR Guide to Managing Strategic Initiatives

HBR Guide to
Remote
Work

HARVARD BUSINESS REVIEW PRESS

Boston, Massachusetts

What You'll Learn

You're likely working remotely more than you used to—maybe a lot more. We're all seeking greater flexibility to balance our jobs and personal lives. Technology has made it easier to meet deadlines and connect outside the office. And companies are realizing, due partly to the Covid-19 pandemic, that many white-collar jobs can be done from just about anywhere.

But working from home, on the road, or in a coffee shop brings unique challenges. You have to rethink many day-to-day aspects of your job, from how to stay productive at your kitchen table to how to collaborate with colleagues you rarely (or never) see in person. If you're a manager, you're dealing with the pressures of supporting a distributed team. Working remotely can also be hard on your mental and emotional health. Isolation, burnout, and exhaustion are all potential risks, as is stress from differing expectations around when the workday actually ends.

Whether you're just setting up your home office or you've worked remotely for years, this guide will help you do your job effectively and solve the problems that come up along the way. You'll learn how to:

- Make yourself indispensable—even when you aren't in the office

- Stay focused despite distractions

- Set boundaries between work and personal time

- Find healthy ways to prevent or deal with burnout

- Balance the demands of parenting and working from home

- Build a collaborative relationship with a virtual boss

- Lead virtual meetings and off-sites effectively

- Be an active, visible participant in video calls

- Help your remote team stay motivated and productive

- Support employees who are struggling to do their jobs remotely

- Resolve conflicts and raise sensitive issues virtually

- Bond with colleagues over a distance

Contents

Contents

SECTION TWO

Navigating Common Challenges

Contents

SECTION FIVE

Being the Boss

SECTION SIX

Solving Problems on a Remote Team

The Art of Being Indispensable— from Wherever You're Working

by Bruce Tulgan

Once, not so long ago, most of us woke up each morning, got dressed, and commuted to work. But times have changed. Today many people are simply rolling out of bed and opening up a laptop (with or without getting dressed). Instead of visiting clients, sitting in conference rooms, and catching colleagues for a quick hallway chat, we're spending our workdays emailing, Zooming, and talking on the phone.

The trend line of working remotely has been rising steadily for decades. As technology has improved, more and more people have begun working from home, on the road, or in organizations with dispersed locations. During the Covid-19 crisis, those numbers skyrocketed and remote work reached a tipping point. Managing work and professional relationships remotely has gone from being a special occasion for most, and routine for only some, to the new normal.

In the process, we've gained some things but lost a lot at the same time. Most people love the flexibility, convenience, and relative comfort of working from home. And while getting rid of our commutes can bring us hours of freed-up time per day, it can be harder to stay motivated and on task when your house is your office.

Also, something valuable disappears when you and your colleagues aren't in the same place at the same time. Working remotely, you miss a lot of unintentional "soft data" exchange—the side glance, the smiling eyes, the feel of excitement or fear in the conference room—things that get noticed only in person. You also miss spontaneous interaction—asking a question or sharing an insight right in the moment—and what I call serendipitous value creation: the creativity and extra effort that often materializes from all that noticing and from the bouncing around of questions, observations, and ideas.

Proximity does matter—not just to how well organizations function but also to how well you're able to do your job. Which has a lot of people wondering: How do you shine at work when there's no actual workplace to do that in? Proving yourself was hard enough when you worked alongside your boss and colleagues. How do you do that now, when you work through virtual meeting rooms, Slack chats, and email?

Positive attitude, hard work, and being great at your job are just table stakes. You don't want to simply meet deadlines and hit targets. You want to be that person everyone trusts to get the right things done, on time, and in the best way possible. You want to be indispensable.

The Indispensable Remote Worker

Even before we hit the remote-work tipping point, doing our jobs had become much harder. In our highly collaborative, matrixed organizations, you likely work with more people than ever, from all over the organization chart—up, down, sideways, and diagonal. You report not just to your direct boss or teammates but also to a seemingly unlimited number of "internal customers." You may field requests from colleagues you don't even know. Other times, *you're* the one who needs to rely on someone else. You are managing a lot of moving parts.

Doing your job from home, you must finesse all this collaboration and communication without the benefit of physical proximity—and reinvent the processes along the way. For all the freedom you may gain from working remotely, you have to work harder than ever to fight overcommitment syndrome. Without the boundaries of the office, it's easy for your workday to have no beginning or end. If you are never at work, you are in danger of being *always* at work. Your inbox has probably exploded, you're having trouble keeping up with texts and voicemail, and even video meetings often drag on longer than the in-person variety. No surprise if you're drop-ping some balls or getting your priorities mixed up—or even losing your motivation to work at all. Add to that the annoying, time-sapping setbacks that come with re-mote work, including technological glitches and distrac-tions in a home office, and getting your work done can be harder than ever.

These are just some of today's challenges—and many are the same whether you're brand-new to long-distance work or a veteran. The good news is that you can over-come some of these obstacles and prove to your man-ager, team, and other colleagues that you're a valuable part of the organization—even as you work remotely. What defines quality work, what effective teams look like, what good management does, and how bosses can help their people grow and flourish haven't changed. Similarly, the ways that people in the workplace prove themselves indispensable are the same things that can guide them as they work remotely. And they all can be done using remote modes like videoconferencing, email, and phone calls.

Productivity and quality are much better measures of performance than working in a particular place dur-ing particular hours. The key to success is focusing on aligned communication, execution for results, and con-tinuous improvement. Here's what that means:

1. **Know what's required of you and what's allowed.** Regularly align with your team on priorities, ground rules, and marching orders. That means engaging in structured dialogue with your boss

and staying in communication with your direct reports. If you are always working within those clear vertical guidelines and parameters, it makes it so much easier to work things out with your lateral and diagonal colleagues.

2. **Understand when to say "no" and how to say "yes."** For any request coming at you—through an email, a text, a Zoom call—clarify every aspect of the request by asking questions and taking notes. Help the asker to fine-tune the ask. That helps you know when to say "no" (or "not yet"). Remember, every "yes" is your opportunity to add value for others and build up your indispensability. So don't waste a single "yes"; follow it with a clear outline of what needs to happen and when, who owns which next steps, and how and when you'll check in with each other along the way.

3. **Decide what you want to be known for.** That means specializing in what you do best and steadily expanding your repertoire. Identify and master best practices, repeatable solutions, and job aids like step-by-step instructions for your customers internal and external.

4. **Finish what you start.** The busier you are, the less you can afford to juggle. If you are always juggling, you will inevitably drop a ball. Break work into small, doable chunks. Find gaps in your schedule for focused execution time so that you can complete projects one by one.

5. **Keep getting better at working together.** Don't focus on building relationships through politicking and personal rapport. Focus your relationship building on the *work*, and the work will go better. When the work goes better, the relationships improve. Write great thank-you notes and channel any discussion of problems into continuous improvement through after-action reviews, to make the next collaboration better.

That's how you build the upward spiral of real influence, the power that people give each other because they want each other to succeed. That's the art of being indispensable at work—even when working remotely.

What This Book Will Do

Think of indispensability as a lens for viewing the advice in this guide. In these pages you'll find best practices, tips, and insights from a variety of experts to help you hone the unique set of skills you'll need for remote working. Their wisdom and experience cover six main topics:

- Getting your work done—stay focused amid distractions, and more

- Navigating common remote work challenges— resolve conflicts or start a new job remotely

- Addressing the emotional and mental health aspects of working remotely—combat burnout, Zoom fatigue, and more

- Handling virtual meetings—elevate your on-camera presence and run an effective meeting

- Being a remote manager—support struggling employees and keep your team motivated

- Solving problems as a remote team—manage across time zones, facilitate collaboration, and more

As you read, remember that the most important thing you can do on the job is be useful to others, adding value in every interaction you have. Whether your workplace is company headquarters or your kitchen table, that's what being indispensable is all about.

———————

Bruce Tulgan is an adviser to business leaders all over the world and a sought-after keynote speaker and seminar leader. He is the founder and CEO of Rainmaker-Thinking, Inc., a management research and training firm, as well as RainmakerLearning, an online training resource. Bruce is the best-selling author of numerous books, including *Not Everyone Gets a Trophy*, *Bridging the Soft Skills Gap*, *The 27 Challenges Managers Face*, and *It's Okay to Be the Boss*. His newest book, *The Art of Being Indispensable at Work*, is available now from Harvard Business Review Press.

Getting Work Done

CHAPTER 1

How to Stay Focused When You're Working from Home

by Elizabeth Grace Saunders

No commute. No drive-by meetings. No dress code. Remote working can seem like a dream—until personal obligations get in the way. These distractions are easy to ignore in an office, but at home it can be difficult to draw the line between personal and professional time.

Consider when you're working on a project and get a call from a friend. You know you need to finish your work, but you feel rude for not talking when *technically* you

Adapted from content posted on hbr.org, September 28, 2017 (product #H03WZ4).

could. Or think about when you're planning your daily to-do list but also need to decide when you'll squeeze in your personal commitments. Taking the time to put a few loads of laundry in the washer midday can seem like a quick task—until you find yourself making up that interrupted work time late at night. In the end, it's never entirely clear when you're really "on" or "off."

As someone who has worked from home for 15 years and been a time management coach for remote workers, I've seen and experienced the good, the bad, and the ugly. I've found that the most focused and effective remote workers set up boundaries for themselves so that they can actually get work done.

Here are some tips for how you can make remote work more productive and satisfying, whether it's an everyday occurrence or an occasional day away from the office.

Establish Working Hours

It may sound silly, but if you want to have a focused day of work, pretend you're not working from home. Before I became a time management coach, my schedule was chaotic. I didn't have a set time that I would be at my computer, and I would often schedule personal appointments or run errands during the day. And since my personal life didn't have boundaries, my work life didn't either. When I was home, I would feel guilty for not checking business email at all hours of the day and night. I never felt that I could truly rest.

But a big shift occurred when I set up "office hours" for working from home (for me, that was about 9 a.m. to 6 p.m. most weekdays) and clarified what was or wasn't acceptable to do during that time. I'd ask myself, "If I was in an office, would I do this task during the day?" If the answer was no, I knew I needed to do the activity before or after office hours. Household chores, errands, and spending time with friends all became activities that needed to happen before or after work. Sure, I would still field an occasional call from a friend during my lunch break, or if I had an urgent task like an emergency car repair, I'd make it happen during the day. But these were exceptions, not the rule. In setting this boundary, I not only created dedicated work time but also found that I could focus on personal items guilt-free "after hours."

Structure Your Day for Success

Maximize the effectiveness of your time at home by structuring it differently than a typical workday. For example, if you work from home only one day a week or on occasion, make it a meeting-free day. If you can't entirely avoid meetings, reserve at least half a day for focused work. Choose a time that works best for you, based on your calendar and your energy level.

Then define one or two key items that you want to accomplish during this time. These could be tasks that require an hour or more of uninterrupted attention, or they could be items that simply require more creative, strategic thinking than you may be able to achieve in the office environment. It's also helpful to shut down your email during this period—or at least stay away from it for an hour at a time. Alert any colleagues of times that you'll be disconnected, so they won't be surprised by a delayed response. (For more tips on setting yourself up for success, see the sidebar "Maintain Momentum While Working from Home.")

MAINTAIN MOMENTUM WHILE
WORKING FROM HOME

Three Tips for Keeping Distractions at Bay
by Carolyn O'Hara

Take Regular Breaks

It may be tempting to work flat out, especially if you're trying to prove that you're productive at home. But it's vital to take breaks. Researchers at a social media company recently tracked the habits of their most productive employees and discovered that the best workers typically worked intently for around 52 minutes and then took a 17-minute break. And these restorative breaks needn't take any particular form—they just need to give your brain an opportunity to briefly recuperate. "The brain is like any other muscle. It needs to rest," says Steven Kramer, a psychologist and coauthor of *The Progress Principle*. "Go for a walk, get some exercise, stretch. Then get back to work."

Stay Connected

Prolonged isolation can lead to weakened productivity and motivation. If you don't have a job that requires face time with others on a daily basis, put in the extra effort to stay connected. Make a point of scheduling regular coffees and meetings with colleagues, clients, and work peers. Get involved with professional organizations. And use online networking sites like LinkedIn to maintain connections with far-flung contacts. Since visibility can be an important factor in who gets promoted (or scapegoated) back at the office, check in as often as you can with colleagues and superiors. "Tell people what you're doing," says Kramer. Share some of the tasks you've accomplished that day. "It's critically important not just for your career but for your psychological well-being," he says.

Celebrate Your Wins

When you're working on your own at home, staying motivated can be difficult, especially when distractions abound. One smart way to maintain momentum is to spend a moment or two acknowledging what you have been able to accomplish that day rather than fixating on what you still need to do. "Take some time at the end of the day to attend to the things that you got done instead of the things you didn't get done," says Kramer. You might also keep a journal in which you reflect on that day's events and note what you were able to check off your to-do list. The daily reminder of what you were able to finish will help create a virtuous cycle going forward.

Carolyn O'Hara is a writer and editor based in New York City. She's worked at *The Week*, *PBS NewsHour*, and *Foreign Policy*. Follow her on Twitter: @carolynohara1.

Adapted from "5 Ways to Work from Home More Effectively," on hbr.org, October 2, 2014 (product #H0111C).

Set Boundaries with Others

To make your efforts stick, be clear with the people who might see your work-at-home days as simply days you're at home. Explain to friends, family, and other acquaintances that the days you're working remotely aren't opportunities for non-work-related activities. For example, if you're home with your spouse, tell them, "I'm planning on being on my computer from 8 a.m. to 5 p.m. today. I'm happy to chat at lunch, but other than that I'll be occupied." Typically, when you set expectations and stick to them (say, really stopping at 5 p.m.), people understand your limits instead of assuming you'll be available. I also recommend having a place where you're away from anyone else who might be home, such as an office or bedroom where you can shut the door and be out of sight.

In situations where you may have unexpected visitors, you'll need to be diplomatic. If a neighbor pops by, be open for a conversation for a few minutes, just as you would with a colleague who stops by your desk. But don't suggest they come in for a cup of coffee or have an extended discussion. Instead, use a graceful exit line like "It was so wonderful to talk with you, but I've got some work to finish up," and then set a time to meet up after hours or on a weekend. Or, if your landlord says he'd like to stop by to do some repairs, offer a time or day that works best for you, rather than letting him take the lead.

If you do need to take on non-work-related requests during the day, set expectations for how much time you have, based on what your schedule is like in the office. For example, if your family asks you to run errands, estimate what you can do during a lunch hour, then commit only to that. For example, say, "I'm happy to pick up the dry cleaning and some milk at lunch, but I won't have time for full-scale grocery shopping until after work." Or break down errands into smaller pieces, such as, "I can drop off the car at the mechanic today, but won't get to calling about the health insurance question until tomorrow."

When you explain your limits, you don't need to do so apologetically. Lay them out factually, having the same respect for your time working from home that you would have if you were on-site. As you consistently communicate and live by these expectations, other people will begin to expect them, and you'll find yourself having more time for focused work.

Elizabeth Grace Saunders is a time management coach and the founder of Real Life E Time Coaching & Speaking. She is the author of *How to Invest Your Time Like Money* and *Divine Time Management*. Find out more at www.RealLifeE.com.

CHAPTER 2

Things to Buy, Download, or Do When Working Remotely

by Alexandra Samuel

Whether you're working from home full-time or simply taking the occasional day away from the office, you'll be most effective if you have the right digital infrastructure. What needs to be in that tool kit depends on the kind of work you do, your personal working style, and your family life. A single software engineer may be able to work from her living room with just her laptop, while a

---

Adapted from content posted on hbr.org, February 4, 2015 (product #H01V3W).

business development professional with young kids will need a private room with a closed door for remote sales calls.

Whatever the circumstances of your remote working arrangement, there are tools and practices that can make your work a lot easier. Here are the tools I recommend based on almost two decades of experience working from home and coffee shops, as both a freelancer and a remote employee:

Software

Document collaboration. Google Drive is already the go-to service for sharing documents with colleagues, but it's doubly useful when you're working remotely. Since you can edit a document on screen in real time, collaborating remotely on a draft agenda or report is just as easy as sitting side-by-side with a paper document—easier, actually, since you'll have all the changes captured by the end of the meeting. You can also use Google Drive or Dropbox to share files and documents that are too large to email.

Note sharing. I use Evernote, a digital notebook application, to keep *all* my notes and web clippings in one place. It's a terrific tool for remote workers, because it keeps notes synced across all devices—so I have access to my notes no matter which laptop I have with me, and if I don't have a laptop handy, they're accessible on my phone and iPad. Evernote also acts as the equivalent of handing a colleague a file of my notes: By inviting someone into a shared notebook, I can easily show work in progress.

Calendaring. If you need to schedule more than the occasional meeting or phone call, set up your calendar with appointment slots that people can book themselves into. You can use Google Calendar's appointment slots, or use a service like Calendly. Set up these appointment windows during a specific chunk of the day or week, and keep your prime concentration hours (whenever they are) blocked off for the kind of uninterrupted work that's hard to get done in the office.

Screen sharing. Even if you aren't doing sales calls, screen sharing on a video call is often the most efficient way to show someone what you're talking about. If you *are* doing sales calls or demos, set up accounts on a couple of different services so that you have a fallback if your usual service doesn't work for whomever you're trying to share with.

Instant messaging. Instant messaging provides many of the benefits of collegiality, without the disruption of a ringing phone or a colleague plopping themselves down at your desk when you're working to a key deadline. Use it to ask someone a quick question or even for a little bit of lightweight socializing that can cut down on the isolation of remote work. It's most effective if you use the same chat service as the lion's share of your colleagues or clients and if you hook it up to your phone's SMS account so that you can read and respond to text messages on your laptop.

Social networking. Even if you've never been a fan of Facebook or Twitter, remote work is a great reason to embrace one or more social networks. It's a way to get some of the ambient sociability and serendipity of working in an office: A five-minute Twitter break can give you a sounding board for a new idea or let you discover that bit of industry news you'd otherwise miss. Choose one social network that will be your virtual watercooler, and drop in at least a couple of times a day so that you're not cut off from the world.

Hardware

All those great cloud-based collaboration tools won't do you a lot of good if you can't get online . . . or turn on your computer. Here's what I recommend keeping on hand so you've always got the access you need.

Your own hotspot. You can't be dependent on the vagaries of coffee shop Wi-Fi, so make sure you have a way of producing your own internet connection anywhere, anytime. That could be as simple as tethering to your phone and using it as your backup connection or buying a USB stick from your wireless company so that you can access cell data from your laptop.

A great headset. Make sure you have a reliable headset for both your home and mobile phone. I've tried a dozen different Bluetooth headsets and headphones, but I prefer using a wired headset so that I don't have to worry about charging and pairing. Using a headset lets you type while you talk—but one of the benefits of remote work is that you don't *have* to sit at your desk. If you've got a call that doesn't require note-taking, your headset lets you go for an energizing walk or gives you the time to clean up your desk (or your kitchen).

A mini power strip. If you carry your own power strip, you'll never find yourself in a café where all the power outlets are already spoken for: Just ask someone if you can unplug their computer so that you can *both* use your power strip. This trick will make you friends in crowded convention centers, too.

Extra cables. Buy an extra charging adapter for your computer and extra cables for all your devices (phone, tablet, etc.). If you keep all your cables in your bag, rather than unplugging them at home every morning, you'll never find yourself stuck without a way to charge.

Battery and car adapter. Carry an external battery that can charge your phone, and make sure you can also charge in the car. Better yet, buy an inverter that will allow you to plug your laptop into your car, so you can always take that crucial sales call from the privacy of your vehicle—without worrying that you'll lose power mid-presentation.

A lightweight laptop. The more mobile you are, the easier it is to work anywhere.

One of the great benefits of living in an online world is the ability to work where and when you want. Harness that power in how you work, and you'll be more productive than any 9-to-5 clock puncher.

———————

Alexandra Samuel is a speaker, writer, and expert on tech-enabled productivity. Alex is the author of *Work Smarter with Social Media* (Harvard Business Review Press, 2015) and (with Robert Pozen) of *Remote, Inc.: How to Thrive at Work...Wherever You Are*. Her class, Work Productivity: Work Smarter with Your Inbox, is available on Skillshare. Follow Alex on Twitter: @awsamuel.

CHAPTER 3

Working from Home When You Have Kids

by Daisy Dowling

You're a parent—and you're working remotely. Maybe it's due to the structure of your new job; maybe it's because of a situation outside your control (like the Covid-19 pandemic); maybe it's part of a corporate work/life initiative; or maybe your company has pulled back on its real estate and expects you to work remotely as a matter of course. Whatever the reason, there are certainly upsides: no commute, no office distractions, no one looking disapprovingly at you when you duck out of the office

---

Adapted from "How to Work from Home When You Have Kids" on hbr.org, September 14, 2017 (product #H03W0V).

for a pediatrician's appointment. Just you, the comfort of home, and the opportunity to spend more time (maybe a *lot* more) with your kids.

Those benefits, however, come with equivalent challenges—particularly at the personal level. How do you stay on the senior leader radar screen? In a 24-7, always-on work culture, how do you avoid the perception—particularly among more senior or traditionally minded colleagues—that you're taking the easy path or have chosen the "parent track"? How do you establish constructive workplace relationships with people you see infrequently? How do you avoid, or work through, the home-life interruptions that can compromise your performance?

Savvy working parents know that it takes more than a home office to make remote work fruitful for their organizations, careers, and families: It takes conscious effort and some specific, effective tactics—which you can start using today.

Keep a firm routine

After years of office life, working remotely can feel wonderfully flexible: Get to your desk at 9:30 a.m. in your pajamas! Feed the baby while on the conference call! But that same lack of traditional workplace boundaries has the potential to erode your motivation and productivity (are you really at your best getting a late start, in sweatpants?). Use your remote work setup to create flexibility that's meaningful to you—to do the kids' morning routine, for example, or to get to soccer games—but keep a firm schedule and habits, too. Start work at the same time each day. Wear what makes you feel sharp and confident. Limit breaks to the same length and frequency as in the office. With a solid routine and the right "guardrails" in place, you'll maximize the feeling of being professional and in control.

Demonstrate your commitment

What your colleagues can't see, they can't appreciate. When working remotely, provide small, clear signals that your commitment and work ethic are unwavering. Send emails first thing in the morning as a means of announcing that you're already up and at it. Let colleagues know that you've read their emails and documents carefully: "Brad, thanks for this—the data on page six will be helpful in our quarterly review process." Take calls in the early morning or late at night as a favor to coworkers in other time zones. These small tactics will let you appear eager, committed, and hardworking—good attributes at any level.

Control the controllables

Pay attention to your physical work environment, and set it up to help you be, and be seen as, professional, focused, and committed. If you can't ensure privacy, that's fine—but alert colleagues on the video call up front that yes, your three-year-old may burst in. Create a professional backdrop for video calls so that no one has to see your kids' ice hockey equipment in the background when you're discussing the quarterly marketing report. Taking charge of these small logistics enhances your working environment and your professional image.

Do a technology audit

Smart use of technology can maximize your efficiency and your connection to colleagues. If your home printer isn't as fast as those in HQ, or you're emailing and calling while everyone else at the office is on Slack, you're missing real opportunity. Partner with the IT team, or with one of the tech-savvy millennials in your department, to help you find and start using the best technological tools. Don't know the best apps for staying in touch and "in the flow" with your company, industry, or function? Ask around to find out.

Allocate 10% of your time to relationship building

In a regular office environment, relationships occur organically—through conversations at the watercooler, in the hallway, at lunch. But when you're working remotely, you will have to create those "connection opportunities" yourself. Call a colleague to check in on their weekend. Email a mentee to ask how her big presentation went. Ensuring that you have regular, informal touch points with everyone on the team—and throughout the organization—will pay big long-term dividends.

Explain it to your kids

Children naturally have difficulty understanding the world of work—what it consists of, what it requires, and what it means. But even very small children can hear that "Mommy works hard all week at the office because I like it, and because it lets me earn money to take care of our family. On Fridays, I still work, but from home so that I can take you to school and we can do fun things together." In doing so, you transmit the values of hard work and responsibility while showing your commitment and love.

Working remotely is a distinct professional skill. As with any other professional skill—like public speaking, negotiations, or financial analysis—it's built over time and through experience, personal reflection, desire for continual improvement, and a lot of hard work. And for any working parent who wants to drive organizational performance, succeed on the job, and raise terrific kids, it's a skill well worth developing.

———————

Daisy Dowling is the founder and CEO of Workparent, the executive coaching and training firm, and the author of *Workparent: The Complete Guide to Succeeding on the Job, Staying True to Yourself, and Raising Happy Kids* (HBR Press, 2021). She is a full-time working parent to two young children. She can be reached at www.workparent.com.

CHAPTER 4

How to Transition Between Work Time and Personal Time

by Elizabeth Grace Saunders

Physical presence doesn't always equate to mental presence. You could be sitting at your desk but more preoccupied about a home repair than the assignment at hand, or you could be at the kitchen table thinking more about the proposal you have to finish than the people eating dinner with you. That's why transitions from work mode to personal mode are so essential. And you have to put

---

Adapted from content posted on hbr.org, April 9, 2020 (product #H05IXU).

especially intentional effort into these transitions when you work from home, because you don't have the natural change-of-context cues.

From my experience as a time management coach, here are some ways to be less distracted and more present, whether you're working or enjoying personal time.

Tell Your Brain It's Time to Work

Mr. Rogers knew how to do transitions right. Many generations of children knew that when he was singing his iconic "It's a Beautiful Day in the Neighborhood," changing his sweater, and then putting on different shoes that it was the start of their time together.

You don't need to sing when you start work (unless you really want to), and you don't need to switch sweaters. But you can have certain things that you do in the same way each morning—even if you work from home. Maybe it's putting your dishes in the dishwasher, turning off the lights that may be on around the house, getting a cup of coffee, and then sitting down at your computer. Or maybe it's doing a quick workout, showering, and then turning to your phone to check email. Whatever works for you, try to do those activities in the same way each day. The point behind this is to prime your brain that this is now work time.

Make a Plan

To increase your productivity and clarity for both work and life outside of work, have a plan for the day. That includes knowing the time of your meetings, deciding what projects you will work on, and being clear on when you will do tasks like answering email. You'll also want to have some plan for your evenings in terms of what you would like to get done or simply do to relax. Knowing that everything has a place, such as a time during your workday when you will work on a presentation or a time in the evening when you can research activities for your kids, helps you to not feel like you *have* to do work during personal time or vice versa.

Another part of your plan should be to designate a few specific times during the day to respond to nonwork messages, texts, and calls. If you aren't in one of those windows, resist the temptation—remember, you're still at work. (To read more about minimizing these distractions, flip back to Chapter 1.)

The most common times people make these daily plans are in the morning at the start of work, as they wrap up their workday, or in the evening before bed. Choose the time that's best for you, and then put a recurring reminder in your calendar to prompt you to build the habit.

Tell Your Brain It's Time to Stop

To make sure you can be fully off the clock later in the evening, have a wrap-up routine that you start at least 30 minutes before you need to end work. This could include doing a final check to make sure that all critical emails have a response; looking over your task list to know that you have completed what's essential; and if you do realize that you will need to work later at night, deciding on exactly what you will complete and when. For example, you might determine, "I will review this proposal for an hour or less starting at 8 p.m." It's good to have that specificity so that you won't have a cloud over your head all evening, knowing that you should probably do some work but without a clear sense of exactly what you will do and when. When the objective and the time frame are clear, you can mentally disconnect until 8 p.m. and then also feel free to completely stop at 9 p.m.

Focus takes intentional effort and can feel difficult at times. But by following these tips, it is possible to be present most of the time when you're working or in your personal time.

Elizabeth Grace Saunders is a time management coach and the founder of Real Life E Time Coaching & Speaking. She is the author of *How to Invest Your Time Like Money* and *Divine Time Management*. Find out more at www.RealLifeE.com.

CHAPTER 5

Staying Motivated in a Remote Job

by Alison Buckholtz

Those of us who work from home might not always admit it, but let's be honest: We often miss the office. Even the too-talkative, too-messy, or too-cutthroat colleagues you willed yourself to ignore when they sat near you can seem endearing when you're toiling away to the ticktock of your kitchen clock.

I've been working from home for almost 15 years. Sometimes it's been across oceans and time zones (we were a military family), and sometimes it's been across town (the office was short on space; I was ruled by my children's schedules; the whole operation was virtual).

Adapted from "How to Work Remotely Without Losing Motivation" on hbr.org, September 22, 2016 (product #H035AL).

At this point in my career as a writer-editor and consultant, I've worked for multinational corporations, international development banks, associations, and nonprofits. I've identified one constant across this long-distance livelihood: No matter how satisfying the to-do list—or how much of an introvert you think you are—working remotely leaves you craving company.

Here's my advice. I don't always follow it, but I'm happier when I do.

Use the time you save on commuting to read a good book

Most people read on the subway—I did when I desked it in a downtown Washington, DC, office for 10 years. Now that I'm based at home, I give myself half an hour at 8 a.m. and 5 p.m. to pick up my paperback. Whatever I absorb usually worms its way into my work, bringing a fresh perspective to the day's writing. Right now I'm halfway through *The Swerve: How the World Became Modern*, by Stephen Greenblatt. Its story of a bibliomaniac who unearths an ancient poem, cracking open the cultural door to the Renaissance, has inspired me with a creative way to write about a venture capital project that's due later this week. Really.

Get out of the house at least once a day

Just as General Stanley McChrystal recommends that you make your bed as soon as you wake up—so that no matter how crappy your day is, you've achieved at least one thing—getting out of the house forces a feeling of accomplishment. Walk around the neighborhood, go to the post office or dry cleaner, sit in a park and look at the trees. Make up an errand if you have to. There's one caveat: Resist the urge to waste $5 on a latte, because it will become a habit. You can dictate how long you'll be away from your work based on deadlines, but even as little as 10 minutes meeting some tangible non-work-related goal can anchor you. You don't have to make your bed unless doing it will keep you from crawling back in.

Make work-together "dates" only if you truly want to

Remember the roommate from hell? The one you were randomly paired with in college based on nothing but a shared birth year? (If you didn't have one, you can borrow mine, who was obsessed with Sheetrock knives.) Meeting up with other work-from-homers to "keep each other company" is like that. If you don't already like the person typing away across the tiny café table, you're not going to bond just because both of you are fleeing daytime doldrums. Eventually, the sound of their fingers hitting the keys will make you want to grab the nearest fork and stab it through their hand. You will long to leave, but you paid too much for that stupid latte.

Make someone else happy

I used to have a picture tacked up on my wall: a cartoon turtle falling from a ceiling, presumably to its death, as it says, "Wheeee, I'm flying!" The caption seemed to be urging the born pessimists among us to look on the bright side of every situation. I try to remember this during the most desperate time of the day, usually around

2 p.m. My eyes are desert-dry and stinging from staring at the computer screen; my body is numb from not moving for hours. I'm on the verge of looking up old boyfriends on Facebook or binging on the year-old, rock-hard brownies at the bottom of the freezer. So here's what I do instead: I call my 98-year-old grandmother. Because I know it will make her happy. As I hang up the phone, a pinprick of light pokes through my mood. I squeeze moisturizing drops into both eyes, close Facebook (again), and get back to work.

Exercise

My treadmill is the best "work-life balance" investment I've ever made. Weather be damned; I'm on it every day. I'm not talking about exercise for weight loss, though that might be a great side benefit. I'm talking about exercise for sanity and productivity—making an effort so taxing that it wipes your mind clean. You can then repopulate your brain with problems and hassles that, with a new perspective, might be solved in a fresh way. This is exercise that allows you to think of nothing except what you are doing at that very moment, that has you sweating through your shirt, that leaves you exhausted and euphoric. The exhaustion won't last, but the euphoria will, and it will see you through the rest of your solitary workday.

When all else fails, remember Maverick

I know a Navy pilot—let's call him Maverick—who deployed to an aircraft carrier for eight months during the Iraq War. If you've never seen anyone land a jet on a carrier in the dead of night, be assured that it's terrifying. But flying missions in war, even landing in darkness, was a pleasure for Maverick compared to the abuse he suffered under a power-hungry boss. Once, when the boss summoned Maverick to his stateroom at 5 a.m. to scream about some perceived misdeed, the boss ended the meeting by throwing his beige rotary phone at Maverick's head. (He missed.) Everything about this story comforts me when I'm hunched over my laptop feeling sorry for myself. I'm not landing a jet on an aircraft carrier at night, during a war. I'm not working at 5 a.m. I'm not ducking a phone wielded by a superior whose judgment it would be treasonous to question.

Speaking of phones, I need to go call my grandmother.

Alison Buckholtz is a writer and editor living in the Washington, DC, area. She is the author of the memoir *Standing By: The Making of an American Military Family in a Time of War.*

Navigating Common Challenges

CHAPTER 6

Working Smoothly with a Virtual Boss

by Keith Ferrazzi

The realities of doing business today often require that employees and their managers work from different locations. When you're not colocated with your boss—especially if you're separated by large distances and time zones—a different set of considerations comes into play, since you'll never casually run into each other in the office hallway or by the watercooler. This was true long before the pandemic set in, and its lessons remain: You've got to change your approach in order to work with and adapt to the realities of having a virtual boss.

Adapted from content posted on hbr.org, December 11, 2014 (product #H01RBP).

Here's the good news: As long as you and your manager can develop trust, keep the communication channels open, and establish clear lines of accountability, there's a good chance that you can work together smoothly. According to our research,[1] the following best practices will help you successfully manage the relationship:

Create a Virtual Contract

First, acknowledge that making your interactions with each other as productive and efficient as possible is going to require a proactive approach. You need to establish the ground rules. How? Start with an email to your boss. Try something like this: "I've attached an article that describes how virtual teams can best work together. Can we discuss it in our upcoming call to see if it's how we want to work together?" What you're doing is setting up a virtual contract that you can both agree on.

Establish Rules for Communication

People on virtual teams misguidedly assume that connecting more often—via more teleconferences, Zoom sessions, emails, and the like—is the answer to the problems of distance. But the result is usually an acute case of screen fatigue and information overload. The real key to managing the relationship with your boss is to set an appropriate cadence of communications so that you're aligned on outcomes. Is it a daily call or a weekly call? Set the frequency that works best for you and your manager, keeping these two rules in mind:

- Specify how quickly you both need to respond to emails and calls.

- Determine what follow-up steps should be taken so that you never let important issues slip through the cracks.

There are other rules to consider as well. Michael Watkins, professor, author, and cofounder of Genesis Advisers, conducted research[2] that found that having regular meetings helped set a rhythm in virtual teamwork. Here's what also worked:

- Sharing meeting agendas ahead of time

- Starting and finishing meetings on schedule

- Starting meetings five minutes late so that parents with kids at home could get them settled

- Rotating meeting times so that people in different time zones could share the load more fairly

Set Clear Goals and Expectations

Think through your personal goals for your work: What would "hitting it out of the park" mean in one month, six months, or a year? Spend some time reflecting, and write down your performance goals and targets. Send them to your boss and have her sign off on them.

Then, in the cadence of meetings that you have already established, have frequent discussions with your boss to make sure you're both checking in on your progress on a regular basis. It's important to establish clear lines of accountability from the start. This means holding yourself to what you said you're going to do by when. Let your manager know that you believe feedback along the way is a gift.

Get Personal

Next, build interpersonal trust. What binds virtual teams of any size together are the personal details—the similarities that lead us to trust the people around us even when they're far away. You can do two things to get personal:

- Send an email to your boss that shares more about who you are. Human beings are social by nature—something that can't be ignored in your virtual relationship. Use the email to tell her about what gives you energy inside and outside the workplace, your hobbies, etc. Ask her to reciprocate. Maybe you'll find some interest that you could participate in together, such as a nonprofit you could volunteer for or a video game session to build teamwork and strategy skills in your off-hours.

- Have regular personal-professional check-ins at the start of meetings. Take no more than 30 seconds to share what's going on personally and professionally in your life, including the happy events (e.g., family and career milestones) and challenges you're facing. Don't dismiss any opportunities to do check-ins; make them important and don't be afraid to show some vulnerability: "Hey, let's do a quick check-in. What's going on?" This simple storytelling and social bonding builds empathy, trust, and camaraderie.

Research conducted by Northeastern University professors[3] found that many employees working from home felt isolated or disconnected, making it difficult for them to develop personal relationships and trust. The study, which predated the Covid-19 pandemic, recommended informal social interactions like the ones described above to increase trust and build stronger connections.

Be Generous

Go overboard to be of service to your boss. Generosity accelerates emotional bonding because it enables you to selflessly focus on your manager's success, which strengthens the relationship.

Start with acts of generosity that are about doing your job extraordinarily well, and then focus on those that go beyond your job. Concentrate on your boss's personal and professional goals to deliver against his or her legacy. Finally, "get personal" and do small things that matter to your manager. Each act builds on the one prior. For example:

- Beat a deadline. (Doing your job extraordinarily well)

- Ask about skunkworks projects that you could get extra credit for working on. (Going beyond your job)

- Ask what legacy your boss wants to leave, and find a way to help him or her achieve it. (Delivering against legacy)

Agree to Be Candid

Don't be conflict-avoidant—it's one of the most destructive attributes of many company cultures. And this is especially true for virtual workers, since you're missing the regular face-to-face interactions that make it easier to develop strong relationships. Transparency and candor build trust, and they should be negotiated in advance, as described earlier, when you set expectations and told your boss that feedback is a gift. Always attack conflicts head-on. Ask for candid feedback, and give feedback too, when appropriate. Nip any problem in the bud.

Tap into Technology

Technology is sometimes labeled as a "distraction" that prevents us from really *connecting*. But when you're working virtually, technology brings you together—especially if everyone can see each other. Viewing people's faces during generous moments such as getting feedback or having a personal-professional check-in only reinforces the good parts of a relationship. Other technologies to consider using include:

- Communication platforms (such as Slack or Microsoft Teams)

- Online scheduling tools (like Doodle or Calendly)

- Cloud document storage and file-sharing tools (such as Dropbox, Box, or Google Drive)

- Project management tools (like Asana, Airtable, Basecamp, or JIRA)

- Document cocreation tools (like Google Docs or Notion)

- Virtual wormholes: 24-7, two-way video connections between two locations, where "virtual office-mates" can see each other continuously

Physical distance is not the death knell to effectively collaborating and forming strong relationships. In fact, it may be irrelevant altogether, because in many organizations where workers are colocated, relationships are often still strained. Why? What's lacking is not physical closeness but emotional closeness, clarity, and alignment. That's why those who work virtually must take a proactive approach to close and overcome strategic and emotional distance. If you truly take these tips to heart, and put clear process and rigor around them, you can have a better, stronger relationship with your boss than the average face-to-face one, regardless of how far apart you work.

Keith Ferrazzi is the founder and chair of Ferrazzi Greenlight, which coaches teams and boards on increasing adaptability and collaboration to capture unexpected growth opportunity and avoid unsuspected risk. He is also a best-selling author on the subject of leadership and teams. His latest book, *Leading Without Authority*, was published in May 2020. *Go Forward to Work* (HBR Press) will be published in Fall 2021.

NOTES

1. Keith Ferrazzi, "Getting Virtual Teams Right," *Harvard Business Review*, December 2014 (product #R1412J), https://hbr.org/2014/12/getting-virtual-teams-right.

2. Michael D. Watkins, "Making Virtual Teams Work: Ten Basic Principles," hbr.org, June 27, 2013 (product #H00AUL), https://hbr.org/2013/06/making-virtual-teams-work-ten.

3. Jay Mulki, Fleura Bardhi, Felicia Lassk, and Jayne Nanavaty-Dahl, "Set Up Remote Workers to Thrive," *MIT Sloan Management Review*, October 1, 2009, https://sloanreview.mit.edu/article/set-up-remote-workers-to-thrive/.

CHAPTER 7

How to Resolve a Conflict with a Remote Colleague

by Amy Gallo

Whether you're exchanging snarky emails, openly disagreeing on a conference call, or giving each other the silent treatment, it's frustrating and painful to fight with a colleague when you're not in the same office or time zone. Without the benefit of face time and forced togetherness, disagreements can easily be left unaddressed or quickly spiral out of control.

What makes conflict from afar so problematic? What's the best way to solve a disagreement with someone who's

Adapted from "Resolve a Fight with a Remote Colleague" on hbr.org, November 30, 2015 (product #H02IU1).

in a different location? And how do you mend the relationship if you can't look the other person in the eye?

What the Experts Say

There are several things that make conflict with a remote colleague challenging, says Mark Mortensen, an associate professor of organizational behavior at INSEAD. "The two main things that get in the way are the lack of shared understanding about how you work and lack of shared identity," he says. When you don't have things in common, you're less likely to give the person the benefit of the doubt. Plus, you don't know how the other person is reacting. Is he being quiet because he's setting aside his feelings, or is he actually stewing? "You're not seeing body language, facial expressions, or hearing voice intonation," says Pamela Hinds, a professor in management science and engineering at Stanford University. "By the time you realize there's a conflict it's often much later than if you were sitting side-by-side." Not all is lost, of course. "The same approaches that work face-to-face also work virtually," says Mortensen. "They're just not going to come as easily." Here are a few things to think about and do differently when tension is brewing with a colleague miles away.

Appreciate the upsides

"There are a lot of upsides to working at a distance," says Mortensen. For example, you often let the small things go. "If we're meeting in person, it might take one look at me to tell that I'm mad, but on the phone, you might just sense that I'm a little more snippy than usual and maybe don't make too much of it," he says. Hinds agrees:

"When you're face-to-face, you tend to thrash it out even if your position isn't that well thought-out." With distance, there is often forgiveness or even just ignorance. "You're less likely to detect annoyance, eye-rolling, and all the other cues that go along with conflict," she says. "The focus tends to be much more on the work and the content of the work."

Give your colleague the benefit of the doubt

Because you don't have a shared context—you're not sitting in the same building, experiencing the same weather, seeing the same things—it's easy to make assumptions about how your colleague feels or why he is acting the way he is. If he's always late to your weekly call, you might presume that he doesn't respect your time or he's not committed to the project. "Our natural reaction is to make personal attributions when something goes wrong, rather than situational attributions," explains Hinds. Instead of thinking the worst about your colleague ("He's so self-absorbed!"), ask yourself what else could be going on. Maybe he's late because he has a regular meeting right before yours that often runs late. Perhaps he's in a bad mood because it's been raining for a week straight where he is. Admit to yourself that you don't know why he's acting the way he is and it may have nothing to do with you.

Move the conversation away from email

Chances are most of your interaction with your remote colleague is over email. This is problematic. A study by Syracuse's Kristin Byron[1] showed what we all know intuitively or have come to learn: Using email generally increases the likelihood of conflict and miscommunication. "We've evolved as humans to pick up on contextual cues. I read your facial expressions. I can tell when you're making a joke or not. When we're not in the same place, I don't have those cues at my disposal," says Mortensen. If you're arguing via email, stop. Pick up the phone and call your colleague, or schedule a time to do a video call. "In order to resolve a conflict, both sides have to understand the other's perspective. That's much harder to do when you can't see each other and the communication isn't synchronous," says Hinds.

Focus on what you have in common

When you're talking with your colleague—by phone or video—start the conversation by highlighting what you have in common. You can talk about how you're both parents of young children, for example, or the college you both went to, or your shared commitment to the job. "Remind people about shared experiences, shared victories, wins. Those will focus people on how we're more similar than not," he says. You don't have to do this overtly by saying, "Hey, we're both moms!" but you can ask about her kids or tell a quick story about yours. "The more you make those things front and center, the more people will feel interdependent on each other," says Mortensen.

See the other side

One of the key skills in resolving a conflict is perspective taking, seeing things from the other person's point of view. Put yourself in her shoes and imagine what she's experiencing. Why might she be upset? What about this situation is frustrating to her? "That will put you in a stronger position to solve the problem, and to mend the fences later on," says Mortensen. You may be working with limited information if you've only met your colleague in person a few times, so ask questions like, "How are you seeing this situation? What might I be missing because I'm here and not there?" You can also encourage your colleague to see things from your vantage point by asking, "If you were me, what would you do?" "This is helpful in any conflict, but especially in distributed teams," says Mortensen.

Consider cultural differences

"Language and cultural differences often compound the issue," says Hinds. It can be hard to know how to handle a conflict with someone who is from a different culture, who may send different emotional cues, or with whom you don't share a language. "If someone says, 'No, it's fine,' it may not mean that. It may mean, 'I'm in complete disagreement with that but I'm not going to say that,'" she says. This is particularly challenging for Americans: "In the U.S., we tend to be relatively direct and we're not as adept at reading more-subtle cues from less direct cultures." If you're not sure how to translate their behavior, find someone who can advise you, perhaps a colleague in the same office or from the same culture.

Bring in someone else if necessary

If you're not able to solve the issue between the two of you, you may need to ask someone else to intervene. "It helps to involve a third person, someone who is not invested in the content of the conflict, to help you reflect and integrate both sides," says Hinds. It doesn't matter where that person is located "as long as the people involved in the conflict agree that the person is reasonable."

Use the fight to strengthen your relationship

One of the benefits of solving a conflict with a remote colleague is that you then have a shared experience. You want disagreements to become water under the bridge, but it's helpful to talk about them as well. "Once you've gotten past the point where the fight's really raw and you can speak about it in a neutral way, you can talk about what happened and that becomes a shared identity," says Mortensen. Hinds agrees: "If the resolution went well and you're both feeling good about it, that's all you need. It's very beneficial to the relationship."

Make a visit

To prevent further conflicts, try to travel to your colleague's office, if that's possible, or invite her to yours. It helps to see "how they interpret you, what it's like to be the person in Japan working with the person in Boston," says Mortensen.

If you can't visit in person, Mortensen suggests spending the first 5–10 minutes of a meeting talking about your work contexts. You can say, "Tell me something I don't know about you or where you're located" or share information about your own situation—what your workspace looks like or what's happening outside. Consider giving your colleague a virtual tour of your office.

Increase informal communication

Research by Mortensen and Hinds[2] shows that casual, unplanned communication dramatically reduces conflict when you're not in the same location. Take advantage of opportunities for informal interactions. Keep your instant messenger open to share personal snippets or jokes throughout the day. Take virtual breaks together, chatting on the phone while you both sip tea. Or you might leave your computer cameras on so that you can see each other throughout the day. "These video links between offices create a shared space and provide more opportunities for these spontaneous—but often very productive—workplace conversations," says Mortensen.

Principles to Remember

Do:

- Highlight anything you have in common— personal or work-related

- Put yourself in your colleague's shoes to better understand how she sees you

- Go visit your colleague in person, if possible

Don't:

- Fight over email; pick up the phone or get on a video call instead

- Assume the worst about your colleague—you don't know why he's behaving the way he is

- Just put the fight behind you; instead, use it as a shared experience to strengthen your relationship

Case Study #1: Pick Up the Phone

Marissa Weiner and her colleague Tara only saw each other in person when Marissa visited their health-care organization's headquarters in Maryland (names and some details have been changed). Tara had a reputation for being difficult to work with, but Marissa wasn't that bothered by her. "I was one of the few people who got along with her. I even defended her to other people who thought she was a pain," says Marissa. But when the two women started working closely on an initiative that Tara was leading, things changed. Tara often sent emails, copying other team members, openly criticizing Marissa's work. They were curt and didn't include any of the usual pleasantries. Tara often sent them late at night, so Marissa would wake up to these harsh notes in her inbox. "At first I let it go," she says. "Part of me knew that she didn't mean to be nasty, that it was a style issue."

But she soon realized that she was stewing about it. "Truthfully, the emails hurt my feelings and I really didn't like being criticized in front of my colleagues," she says. On her next trip to Maryland, she asked Tara out to dinner. "I was very direct and told her that her emails were bothering me, that it felt like she didn't respect my work." Tara was taken by surprise. She said she hadn't intended to offend Marissa.

She apologized and vowed to be more careful, but things didn't improve immediately. "She still sent those emails, but I would point it out to her right away. Instead of emailing her back, I would pick up the phone. When she can hear my voice, she is far less defensive," she says.

Marissa admits that it took a lot of effort to do this, but "it was better than feeling resentful. I couldn't change her behavior but I could explain how her behavior was impacting me."

They are still working on the project, and Marissa says it's going much more smoothly. "We understand each other better, and I've developed tactics to work with her. She still has a reputation, but she also has a lot to contribute."

Case Study #2: Don't Assume Your Colleague Is Disrespecting You

When Leah Briar, the New York–based sales development director of a West Coast media company, was put on an important research project with Irina, a colleague who worked at headquarters in San Francisco, she knew it was going to be a challenge (names and some details have been changed). Leah had always been bothered by Irina's tone of voice on the phone. "I never really liked her communication style. She has a weird phone cadence and pauses and hesitates a lot," she explains.

Previously Leah had "just dealt with it." But when she and Irina starting speaking daily in order to complete the research for a major event that was only several weeks away, her frustration grew and she didn't hide it. During Irina's pauses, she would often snap, "Do you understand what I'm saying? Are you there? Are we on the same page?" And Irina would snap back, "Yes, I'm here."

"What I found infuriating was that she wasn't clueing me in to her process; she wasn't narrating what she was going through, so I was left in the dark," Leah recalls.

Finally, after a week of tense calls, she suggested they try a video call and Irina agreed. "She was definitely feeling exasperated too. She couldn't understand why I was being so impatient."

The change made all the difference. "I could see her pauses physically. I saw that she was hearing me and paying attention; she wasn't multitasking or distracted. She was just thinking." Irina seemed much more relaxed too. "Her tone of voice completely changed."

Amy Gallo is a contributing editor at *Harvard Business Review* and the author of the *HBR Guide to Dealing with Conflict*. She writes and speaks about workplace dynamics. Watch her TEDx talk on conflict and follow her on Twitter: @amyegallo.

NOTES

1. Daniel Goleman, "E-Mail Is Easy to Write (and to Misread)," *New York Times*, October 7, 2007, https://www.nytimes.com/2007/10/07/jobs/07pre.htm.

2. Pamela J. Hinds and Mark Mortensen, "Understanding Conflict in Geographically Distributed Teams: The Moderating Effects of Shared Identity, Shared Context, and Spontaneous Communication," *Organization Science*, June 1, 2005, https://pubsonline.informs.org/doi/abs/10.1287/orsc.1050.0122.

CHAPTER 8

4 Ways to Demonstrate Your Value—Remotely

by Elizabeth Grace Saunders

When you work from home, you don't have the visibility with your colleagues and managers that you normally would. In an office, you might have informal interactions with these people multiple times a day. Now, if you don't have a meeting on their calendar, you may wonder if they remember your presence—and more important, your value to the organization.

There are ways that you can make yourself and your accomplishments more visible to your organization,

---

Adapted from "5 Ways to Demonstrate Your Value—Remotely" on hbr.org, June 1, 2020 (product #H05NYG).

even when you're not in the same building. The following four suggestions are concrete steps that you can focus on right here, right now, to increase your odds of thriving in your job and demonstrating your value while working remotely.

Do Your Work

Getting your work done is always a good idea. But it's especially so in times of uncertainty. During the Covid-19 pandemic, many people became accustomed to working from home for an extended period of time. As a time management coach, I got the sense from my clients that there was a grace period in the crisis's early stages, when everyone was adjusting to working remotely. Managers were more forgiving if there was a dip in productivity or missteps here and there. But higher standards of output have returned. If you haven't done so already, put a system in place for keeping track of your tasks and ticking them off, even if your schedule is modified because you have other responsibilities at home.

Tell Others

I don't recommend that you give yourself a shout-out at every single meeting, and I definitely don't advise that you take undue credit for others' work. But if you have accomplished something significant, share it. That could look like covering a few highlights of your work with your boss each week, either in your one-on-one or through email. Or speaking up in a meeting to share about what your team is doing. Or even giving a presentation on some best practices that could help other colleagues in a similar role. Focus on not only what you did but how it produced positive results for your organization. This is not bragging; it's simply informing others about how, even though they might not see you working, you're getting great things accomplished. And this gives you increased visibility across the organization as people understand the role that you fill and the value you add.

Play Nicely

With my clients, one of their least-favorite ways to spend their time is brokering arguments between people on their team. It drains energy, and they generally consider it a waste of time.

You want to be seen not only as a valuable individual contributor but also as someone who elevates the entire team. Try to work out differences with your colleagues on your own, without getting your manager involved. If you feel you absolutely must escalate a disagreement to your boss, do so minimally and only when it's appropriate. Taking this approach to conflict shows that you have the capability to communicate and collaborate with others well, and it keeps your boss from being hesitant to put you on teams because they're concerned you won't play well with others.

Spread Positivity

It's easy to focus on our anxieties, on the uncertain future, and on all the things we can't control. Try something different. When you're chatting before the start of a meeting or sending an email, mention something uplifting. That could be the birds you saw on a walk, the silly things your kids did, or a book you're reading. If needed, come up with some varied subjects in advance each day. Whatever you focus on expands, so expand good in the lives of your coworkers.

And if you're comfortable, be funny. Laughter and positive energy draw teams together and make people feel good about being around you.

Certain things about work will always be out of your control. However, if you follow the pieces of advice above, you will do what you can to make the most impact and get credit for it within your current role. And you'll make a positive impression in the process.

––––––––––––

Elizabeth Grace Saunders is a time management coach and the founder of Real Life E Time Coaching & Speaking. She is the author of *How to Invest Your Time Like Money* and *Divine Time Management*. Find out more at www.RealLifeE.com.

CHAPTER 9

Starting a New Remote Job

by Art Markman

Most of us know how to start a job in person. But what if your new position is remote? When you aren't in an office, there are certain benefits you won't have, such as on-site onboarding or meeting your coworkers face-to-face. And that means your early days at the company could be especially tricky.

You should always be proactive in getting acclimated to a new role, but when you're remote, it's especially imperative that you take an active approach to getting up to speed. Here are five things you can do to fill the gaps and minimize the bumps as you transition into the new job.

Adapted from "Starting a New Job—Remotely" on hbr.org, May 4, 2020 (product #H05LLQ).

Schedule a Lot of Brief Check-ins with Colleagues

One of the hardest things about starting with a new company is that each organization has a culture of its own. And that culture is often made up of unspoken goals and norms and wrapped up in a unique language that members of your new team speak with ease. In my consulting work, I've frequently been baffled by terms that employees use inside companies but that have no meaning outside it.

You may have gotten a glimpse of this culture when you interviewed for your new position—either in person or remotely. (For tips on landing a job, see the sidebar "Advice for Remote Job Interviews.") But you learn the more subtle aspects of the workplace through everyday interactions with colleagues, hearing conversations and having discussions about what other people are working on. You pick up on workplace jargon and you surmise from these conversations what activities are valued and what styles of work are appreciated.

Under normal circumstances, these interactions are a natural part of being in the office. But as a remote worker, you're going to have to manufacture them. Reach out to your new colleagues and set up quick, 10- to 15-minute one-on-one discussions. These can happen by phone or video and shouldn't be one-offs. Meet with your colleagues regularly to mimic the short, informal interactions you'd have in person. Use these conversations as a chance to ask questions you may have about your current projects, but make sure to ask people what they are working on too, so they have a chance to describe their tasks. Pay attention to any implicit statements about what they think is most important.

Rapidly Assemble Your Mentoring Team

Throughout your career, you need a team of people who will mentor you. There are two types of mentors who are particularly important inside your current company. The first is someone who knows how things get done in the firm and who can help you to navigate the variety of procedures you have to go through to do everything from getting reimbursed for expenses to accessing equipment. The second is a person who is well-connected throughout the organization and can introduce you to people you need to know.

Ordinarily, you can afford to develop these relationships slowly. When you start working for a company remotely, though, you want to identify initial candidates to play these roles for you as quickly as possible. You can't just make your way around the office finding colleagues you know who might point you in the right direction. Instead, your requests are likely to involve emails or queries via instant message, and those responses can be slow. If you put some good mentors in place quickly, you make it easier to be productive quickly.

However, don't feel like you have to commit to having these people as mentors throughout your tenure at the company. The downside to choosing quickly is that you may settle on someone who is available but not the perfect fit. As you get to know the organization better, you may choose to reach out to other people to be your guides. But having someone early on is better than having nobody.

Announce Yourself as New

When you start a job in an office, people tend to notice that they see a new face around the halls. And under normal circumstances, you can expect people to introduce themselves and even offer help.

That is not going to happen when you're the new person in the virtual office. Ideally, your new manager will introduce you, but you'll likely "meet" many of your new colleagues as one of a sea of faces in a virtual meeting. That means you need to be intentional about getting acquainted with your coworkers. If there is a team meeting, see if you can get a moment to introduce yourself. But also let people know who you are in forums like Slack and by sending some brief emails to other people in your unit. That may be hard if you don't like to call attention to yourself, but you want to let folks know that you're new and that you would appreciate their help in getting settled. Many of your colleagues would like to welcome you; they just need more-explicit reminders to do so than they might otherwise.

Ask for Help

In the office, colleagues often pick up on a quizzical facial expression or tone of voice and may offer assistance if they think you need it. On video and phone meetings, it'll be hard for people to see if you are confused or not keeping up. As a rule, when there is something you need, say so.

ADVICE FOR REMOTE JOB INTERVIEWS

by Amy Gallo

As working from home has become more common, so has the remote job interview. All of the standard advice about how to perform well during an interview still applies—prepare, make a good first impression, connect your experience to the job's requirements—but you'll also need to think about other aspects as well:

Confirm and test technology. When the interview is scheduled, ask what video platform they'll be using and then spend time familiarizing yourself with how it works, especially if you'll need to use any features like screen sharing. Test out the link ahead of time. Be sure you have a way to reach the interviewer in case the technology fails.

Plan your appearance. Your goal is to look professional. You don't necessarily need to wear a suit jacket—that could look awkward under the circumstances—but you don't want to wear a sweatshirt either. Choose a neutral background for your interview (it probably goes without saying to avoid one of those virtual beach backgrounds).

Rehearse ahead of time. Experiment with how you might answer common questions, and rehearse in the spot where you plan to do the interview so that you can see how you look on camera. If you can't stop looking at yourself when you practice, you might want to close the window with your image in it.

(continued)

ADVICE FOR REMOTE JOB INTERVIEWS

Have a positive mindset. During the interview, you won't be getting the same level of nonverbal information from the interviewer. Claudio Fernández-Aráoz, an executive fellow at Harvard Business School and the author of *It's Not the How or the What but the Who*, points out there's lots of research that shows that when we don't have feedback, we tend toward a negativity bias and assume things aren't going well. Experiment ahead of time with staying positive and assuming the best is happening.

Exaggerate your emotions a bit. For the same reason, you want to practice being emotive during the interview. "Unless you have a sophisticated set of earphones, the audio gets compressed and you lose many of the undertones, which convey emotions," Fernández-Aráoz explains. "So you need to exaggerate those a bit." He suggests practicing with a friend on video to "get some feedback about the setting, your tone, and your body language." Your goal is to appear natural and at ease.

Amy Gallo is a contributing editor at *Harvard Business Review* and the author of the *HBR Guide to Dealing with Conflict*. She writes and speaks about workplace dynamics. Watch her TEDx talk on conflict and follow her on Twitter: @amyegallo.

Adapted from "How to Nail a Job Interview—Remotely" on hbr.org, June 22, 2020 (product #H05OXQ).

You might be worried that your colleagues won't want to help. After all, everyone already has a lot going on. Quite a bit of research[1] by Vanessa Bohns, associate professor of organizational behavior at Cornell's ILR School, and her colleagues suggests that people are often much more willing to help than you believe they will be. So, don't wait for offers of assistance. Ask for what you need.

Keep a Daily Diary

When you're in the office, it's easy to take care of problems as they arise. You can often just get up from your desk and find someone to help you solve it. When you're working at home, if you dash off an email asking for an answer, your request may get lost in the noise. And if it's a small issue, you may even forget to follow up.

End each day by going back through your schedule and making some notes about how things went. Write down the tasks you accomplished and the obstacles you faced. If there are particular issues that are still unresolved, highlight them. Then when you have your next meeting with a supervisor or colleague, raise those issues and ask for their perspective.

Your memory for what happens each day is strongest around things that are compatible with your general script about how work is supposed to go. That means that you are least likely to remember the novel aspects of your new workplace—which are precisely the elements that you need the most help with. Writing down the events of your day while they are still fresh in your mind is a great way to overcome this bias.

It's never easy being the new person on a team, and working remotely certainly makes it tougher. But by being proactive you can more smoothly acclimate to the new team and organization and prove your value more quickly.

———————

Art Markman, PhD, is the Annabel Irion Worsham Centennial Professor of Psychology, Human Dimensions of Organizations, and Marketing at the University of Texas at Austin and executive director of the IC² Institute. He has written more than 150 scholarly papers on topics including reasoning, decision making, and motivation. His most recent book is *Bring Your Brain to Work: Using Cognitive Science to Get a Job, Do It Well, and Advance Your Career* (HBR Press).

NOTE

1. Vanessa K. Bohns and Francis J. Flynn, "'Why Didn't You Just Ask?" Underestimating the Discomfort of Help-Seeking," *Journal of Experimental Social Psychology* (January 2010). https://doi.org/10.1016/j.jesp.2009.12.015.

Caring for Your Mental and Emotional Health

CHAPTER 10

3 Tips to Avoid Work-from-Home Burnout

by Laura M. Giurge and Vanessa K. Bohns

In 2020, millions of people started working from home for the first time, amid the Covid-19 pandemic. Not surprisingly, this has made some employers concerned about maintaining employee productivity. But the bigger risk with our new ways of working is a longer-term one: employee burnout.

The risk is substantial. The lines between work and nonwork time and space have been blurred in new and unusual ways, and many remote employees—especially

---

Adapted from "3 Tips to Avoid WFH Burnout" on hbr.org, April 3, 2020 (product #H05IX0).

those who worked from home for the first time during the pandemic—likely struggle to preserve healthy boundaries between their professional and personal lives. To signal their loyalty, devotion, and productivity, they may feel they have to work all the time. Afternoons will blend with evenings; weekdays will blend with weekends; and little sense of time off will remain.

Lots of research suggests that drawing lines between our professional and personal lives is crucial, especially for our mental health.[1] But it's difficult, even in the best of circumstances. In no small measure, that's because the knowledge economy has radically transformed what it means to be an "ideal worker."

Our research has shown that people often unintentionally make it hard for their supervisors, colleagues, and employees to maintain boundaries. One way they do so is by sending work emails outside regular office hours. In five studies involving more than 2,000 working adults, we found that senders of after-hours work emails underestimate how compelled receivers feel to respond right away, even when such emails are not urgent, with negative consequences on their well-being.

So how can employees continue to compartmentalize their work and nonwork lives, given the extraordinary situation that so many of us are in today? How can we "leave our work at the door" if we are no longer going out the door? What can employers, managers, and coworkers do to help one another cope and thrive in the contemporary workplace?

Based on our research and the wider academic literature, here are some recommendations:

Maintain Physical and Social Boundaries

In a classic paper,[2] Blake Ashforth, of Arizona State University, described the ways in which people demarcate the transition from work to nonwork roles via "boundary-crossing activities." Putting on your work clothes, commuting from home to work—these are physical and social indicators that something has changed. You've transitioned from "home you" to "work you."

Try to maintain these boundaries when working remotely. In the short term, it may be a welcome change not to have to catch an early train to work or to be able to spend all day in your pajamas—but both of those things are boundary-crossing activities that can do you good, so don't abandon them altogether. Put on your work clothes every morning—casual Friday is fine, of course, but get yourself ready nonetheless. And consider replacing your morning commute with a walk to a nearby park, or even just around your apartment, before sitting down to work.

Maintain Temporal Boundaries as Much as Possible

Maintaining temporal boundaries is critical for well-being and engagement. This is particularly true for employees—and their colleagues—who face the challenge of integrating childcare or eldercare responsibilities during regular work hours. It's challenging even for employees without children or other family responsibilities, thanks to the mobile devices that keep our work with us at all times.

Sticking to a 9-to-5 schedule may prove unrealistic. Employees need to find work "time budgets" that function best for them. They also need to be conscious and respectful that others might work at different times than they do. For some it might be a child's nap; for others it might be when their partner is cooking dinner. Employees with or without children can create intentional work time budgets by adding an "out of office" reply during certain hours of the day to focus on work. A less-extreme reply could be to just let others know that you might be slower than usual in responding, decreasing expectations for others and yourself. You could also add a small note in your email footer indicating that while you might reply outside normal office hours, you have no expectation that anyone else will do the same.

Creating clear temporal boundaries often depends on the ability to coordinate one's time and availability with others'. This calls for leaders to aid employees in structuring and managing the pace of work. That might mean regularly holding virtual check-in meetings with employees, or providing them with tools to create virtual coffee breaks or workspaces.

Focus on Your Most Important Work

While working from home, employees often feel compelled to project the appearance of productivity, but this can lead them[3] to work on tasks that are more immediate instead of more important—a tendency that research[4] suggests is counterproductive in the long run, even if it might benefit productivity in the short run. Employees, particularly those facing increased workloads as they juggle family and work tasks, should pay attention to prioritizing important work.

Working all the time, even on your most important tasks, isn't the answer. According to some estimates,[5] the typical knowledge worker is productive only three hours every day, and these hours should be free of interruptions or multitasking. Even before Covid-19, employees found it difficult to carve out three continuous hours to focus on their core tasks. With work and family boundaries being removed, employees' time and attention have never been more fragmented.

Employees who feel "on" all the time are at a higher risk of burnout when working from home than if they were going to the office as usual. In the long term, trying to squeeze in work and email responses whenever we have a few minutes to do so—during nap time, on the weekend, or by pausing a movie in the evening—is not only counterproductive but also detrimental to our well-being and even the well-being of others. We all need to find new ways to carve out nonwork time and mental space—and help others do the same.

These are just a few recommendations that can help workers maintain boundaries between their work and personal lives and thereby avoid burnout in the long run. Employees, with the support of their managers, will need the flexibility to experiment with how to make their circumstances work for them.

Laura M. Giurge is a postdoctoral research fellow at London Business School and the Barnes Research Fellow at

the Wellbeing Research Centre at the University of Oxford. You can read more about her ongoing work at www
.lauramgiurge.com.

Vanessa K. Bohns is an associate professor of organizational behavior at the ILR School at Cornell University. You can read more about her research in her forthcoming book, *You Have More Influence Than You Think*, and at www.ilr.cornell.edu/people/vanessa-bohns.

NOTES

1. Scott Schieman, "Gender, Dimensions of Work, and Supportive Coworker Relations," *Sociological Quarterly* 47, no. 2 (December 2016): 195–214. https://www.tandfonline.com/doi/full/10.1111/j.1533
-8525.2006.00043.x.

2. Blake E. Ashforth, Mel Fugate, and Glen E. Kreiner, "All in a Day's Work: Boundaries and Micro Role Transitions," *Academy of Management Review* 25, no. 3 (July 2000): 472–491. https://www
.researchgate.net/profile/Glen_Kreiner/publication/228079856_All_
in_A_Day%27s_Work_Boundaries_and_Micro_Role_Transitions/
links/542f1f720cf27e39fa994fa0/All-in-A-Days-Work-Boundaries
-and-Micro-Role-Transitions.pdf.

3. Meng Zhu, Yang Yang, and Christopher K. Hsee, "The Mere Urgency Effect," *Journal of Consumer Research* 45, no. 3 (October 2018): 673–690, https://academic.oup.com/jcr/article-abstract/45/3/
673/4847790.

4. Diwas S. KC, Bradley R. Staats, Maryam Kouchaki, and Francesca Gino, "Task Selection and Workload: A Focus on Completing Easy Tasks Hurts Long-Term Performance," Harvard Business School, working paper 17-112 (June 25, 2017), https://www.hbs.edu/faculty/
Publication%20Files/17-112_54fdf950-a08d-4ba8-a718
-1150dc8916cb.pdf.

5. "How Many Productive Hours in a Workday? Just 2 Hours, 23 Minutes . . . ," vouchercloud, https://www.vouchercloud.com/
resources/office-worker-productivity.

CHAPTER 11

Resilience Is About How You Recharge, Not How You Endure

by Shawn Achor and Michelle Gielan

As constant travelers and parents of a two-year-old, we sometimes fantasize about how much work we can do when one of us gets on a plane, undistracted by phones, friends, and *Finding Nemo*. We race to get all our groundwork done: packing, going through TSA, doing a last-minute work call, calling each other, boarding the plane. Then, when we try to have that amazing work

---

Adapted from content posted on hbr.org, June 24, 2016 (product #H02Z3O).

session in flight, we get nothing done. Even worse, after refreshing our email or reading the same studies over and over, we are too exhausted when we land to soldier on with the emails that have inevitably piled up.

Why should flying deplete us? We're just sitting there doing nothing. Why can't we be tougher—more resilient and determined in our work—so that we can accomplish all of the goals we set for ourselves? Based on our current research, we have come to realize that the problem is not our hectic schedule or the plane travel itself; the problem comes from a misunderstanding of what it means to be resilient, and the resulting impact of overworking.

We often take a militaristic, "tough" approach to resilience and grit. We imagine a marine slogging through the mud, a boxer going one more round, or a football player picking himself up off the turf for one more play. We believe that the longer we tough it out, the tougher we are, and therefore the more successful we will be. However, this entire conception is scientifically inaccurate.

The very lack of a recovery period is dramatically holding back our collective ability to be resilient and successful. Research has found[1] that there is a direct correlation between lack of recovery and increased incidence of health and safety problems. And lack of recovery—whether by disrupting sleep with thoughts of work or having continuous cognitive arousal by watching our phones—is costing our companies $62 billion a year[2] (that's billion, not million) in lost productivity.

And just because work stops, it doesn't mean we are recovering. We "stop" work sometimes at 5 p.m., but then we spend the night wrestling with solutions to problems, talking about projects over dinner, and falling asleep

in bed for hours, unable to fall asleep because your brain is thinking about work. If you lie in bed for eight hours, you may have rested, but you can still feel exhausted the next day. That's because rest and recovery are not the same thing. Stopping does not equal recovering.

If you're trying to build resilience at work, you need adequate internal and external recovery periods. As researchers Fred Zijlstra, Mark Cropley, and Leif Rydstedt wrote in a paper published in 2014:[3] "Internal recovery refers to the shorter periods of relaxation that take place within the frames of the workday or the work setting in the form of short scheduled or unscheduled breaks, by shifting attention or changing to other work tasks when the mental or physical resources required for the initial task are temporarily depleted or exhausted. External recovery refers to actions that take place outside of work— e.g., in the free time between the workdays, and during weekends, holidays, or vacations." If after work you lie around on your bed and get riled up by political commentary on your phone or get stressed thinking about decisions regarding how to renovate your home, your brain has not received a break from high mental arousal states. Our brains need a rest as much as our bodies do.

If you really want to build resilience, you can start by strategically stopping. Give yourself the resources to be tough by creating internal and external recovery periods. In her book *The Future of Happiness*, based on her work at the Yale School of Management, Amy Blankson describes how to strategically stop during the day by using technology to control overworking. She suggests downloading an app to track how many times you turn on your phone. The average person turns on their phone 150 times every day. If every distraction took only one minute (which would be seriously optimistic), that would account for two and a half hours each day.

You can use certain apps to create tech-free zones by strategically scheduling automatic airplane modes. In addition, you can take a cognitive break every 90 minutes to recharge your batteries. Rather than having lunch at your desk, spend time outside or talk with your friends—but not about work. Take all of your paid time off, which not only gives you recovery periods but raises your productivity and likelihood of promotion.

As for us, we've started using our plane time as a work-free zone, and thus time to dip into the recovery phase. The results have been fantastic. We are usually tired already by the time we get on a plane, and the cramped space and spotty internet connection make work more challenging. Now, instead of swimming upstream, we relax, meditate, sleep, watch movies, journal, or listen to entertaining podcasts. And when we get off the plane, instead of being depleted, we feel rejuvenated and ready to return to the performance zone.

Shawn Achor is the *New York Times*–best-selling author of *Big Potential, The Happiness Advantage*, and *Before Happiness*. He serves as the Chief Experience Officer for BetterUp. His TED talk is one of the most popular, with more than 11 million views. He has lectured or researched at over a third of the *Fortune* 100 companies and in 50 countries, as well as for the NFL, Pentagon, and White House. Shawn led a series of courses on "21 Days to Inspire Positive Change" with the Oprah Winfrey Network.

Michelle Gielan, a national CBS News anchor turned positive psychology researcher at the University of Pennsylvania, is the best-selling author of *Broadcasting Happiness*. She has spent the past decade researching the link between optimism and success and has worked with hundreds of organizations, including Google, American Express, and AT&T, on how to create a positive culture to drive business results.

NOTES

1. Judith K. Sluiter, "The Influence of Work Characteristics on the Need for Recovery and Experienced Health: A Study on Coach Drivers," Ergonomics 42, no. 4 (November 2010): 573–583. https://www.tandfonline.com/doi/abs/10.1080/001401399185487

2. American Academy of Sleep Medicine, "Insomnia Costing U.S. Workforce $63.2 Billion a Year in Lost Productivity, Study Shows," ScienceDaily, September 2011, https://www.sciencedaily.com/releases/2011/09/110901093653.htm.

3. F. R. H. Zilstra, M. Cropley, and L. W. Rydstedt, "From Recovery to Regulation: An Attempt to Reconceptualize 'Recovery from Work,'" *Stress and Health* 30 (2014): 244–252, https://www.academia.edu/7904615/SPECIAL_ISSUE_PAPER_From_Recovery_to_Regulation_An_Attempt_to_Reconceptualize_Recovery_from_Work_Introduction.

CHAPTER 12

5 Tips to Reduce Screen Time While You're Working from Home

by Elizabeth Grace Saunders

Pre-coronavirus, you likely thought that you spent almost all of your workday at the computer. But little did you know that you could spend so much more. Between commutes, formal meetings, drive-by chats, watercooler talks, coffee breaks, and lunches, you had many opportunities throughout your day to give your eyes a break from your screen and detach from the digital realm.

Adapted from "5 Tips to Reduce Screen Time While You're WFH" on hbr.org, May 15, 2020 (product #H05MBT).

Now, with more of your time spent working at home and those natural respites eliminated, there's little to no break from the connection to technology. In particular, video calls add an extra layer of fatigue. Having to focus on multiple faces simultaneously, while also being conscious that everyone can see you, creates an added layer of mental and emotional exhaustion that wouldn't be experienced as acutely in an in-person setting. The extra time in front of the computer can also cause eye strain and muscle fatigue because you need to hold your body rigid for hours to stay inside a camera's range.

To help my time-management-coaching clients maintain and regain energy, we've been working on ways that they can reduce or eliminate technology throughout their day. Here are a few strategies that have been most effective.

Don't Default to Video Calls

Video chat apps are wonderful tools when you are trying to replicate in-person interactions as closely as possible. But the level of intensity video calling offers isn't necessary for many communications. If a phone call would work fine for a conversation, use that. If you can efficiently communicate what you need via email or through updating a shared document or task management system, take that approach. Just because you *can* use video doesn't mean you *should*.

Limit Your Meeting Time

In normal circumstances, setting aside blocks of time to get work done is a good idea. But if you find virtual meetings draining, this practice is even more essential for you as you work remotely. Block out time on your schedule when you're not available for meetings so that you can temper how much virtual communication you have each day. That could look like setting aside most of a morning or afternoon as a meeting-free time or blocking out a few one-hour chunks of time throughout the day to detach and focus on other work.

Choose Physical over Digital

To deal with the increased time in front of a screen both on and off the clock, look for ways that you can take the low-tech route. Brainstorming for an article? Write out your thoughts on paper. Creating a road map for a big project? Sketch the initial draft on a whiteboard. Reading a book? Pick up a print copy. Exercising? Go outside on a run. Anytime you can reasonably choose a physical option over a digital one, take it. I find that stepping away from my computer not only offers a digital break but also helps me to be more creative.

Move as Much as Possible

To counteract the fatigue caused by sitting rigidly in front of your computer, move around as much as you can. In between meetings, take a walk to the kitchen to refill your water or coffee. When you need a quick break, do a few simple movements like rolling your shoulders to get the blood flowing. If you have a standing desk, move it up and down so you're able to both sit and stand throughout the day. If you don't have a standing desk, put your computer on a high counter or bureau to get an opportunity to stretch your legs. And if you're on a normal phone call and don't need to be taking notes or looking at documents while you talk, consider standing up or walking back and forth during the conversation.

Take Tech-Free Breaks

Although it may feel more "efficient" to eat lunch at your computer, your brain will thank you for taking a break from the screen. Eat lunch while chatting with your family members in the kitchen, looking out a window, or reading a physical book. Stepping away from technology not only gives your brain a break but also gives you the added bonus of perspective. I find that even when I take a short lunch of just 15 to 20 minutes—when I simply eat without doing anything else—I feel more peaceful at the end than I did before. I also tend to have a clearer sense of the big picture of what's occurring in my life and work.

Another practice that's benefiting me as well as many of my clients is post-work outdoor physical activity. This includes taking a walk, playing basketball in a driveway, gardening, or anything else that gets you active. This split from the digital world refreshes your brain and helps to create some separation from the end of your workday and the beginning of your personal time.

The pandemic may have helped us learn new ways of working and communicating (whether we wanted to or not), but it also introduced new digital pain points into our workdays. Our increased reliance on screens is certainly among them. These strategies can help you counter that load and reduce digital fatigue.

Elizabeth Grace Saunders is a time management coach and the founder of Real Life E Time Coaching & Speaking. She is the author of *How to Invest Your Time Like Money* and *Divine Time Management*. Find out more at www.RealLifeE.com.

CHAPTER 13

How to Combat Video Call Fatigue

by Liz Fosslien and Mollie West Duffy

If constant video calls leave you more exhausted at the end of your workday than you used to be, you're not alone. In the early months of the coronavirus pandemic, as remote work accelerated, mentions of "Zoom fatigue" popped up on social media and Google searches for the same phrase spiked.

Why do we find video calls so draining? There are a few reasons.

In part, it's because they force us to focus more intently on conversations in order to absorb information. Think of it this way: When you're sitting in a conference

---

Adapted from "How to Combat Zoom Fatigue" on hbr.org, April 29, 2020 (product #H05L9B).

room, you can rely on whispered side exchanges to catch you up if you get distracted, or you can ask quick, clarifying questions. During a video call, however, it's impossible to do this unless you use the private chat feature or awkwardly try to find a moment to unmute and ask a colleague to repeat themselves.

The problem isn't helped by the fact that video calls make it easier than ever to lose focus. We've all done it— decided that, why yes, we absolutely can listen intently, check our email, text a friend, and post a smiley face online within the same 30 seconds. Except, of course, we don't end up doing much listening at all when we're distracted. And many of our work-from-home situations add fuel to the fire. We're no longer just dialing into one or two virtual meetings. We're also continually finding polite new ways to ask our loved ones not to disturb us, or tuning them out as they army-crawl across the floor to grab their headphones off the dining table. For those who don't have a private space to work, it is especially challenging.

Finally, Zoom fatigue stems from how we process information over video. On a video call the only way to show we're paying attention is to look at the camera. But in real life, how often do you stand within three feet of a colleague and stare at their face? Probably never. This is because having to engage in a "constant gaze" makes us uncomfortable—and tired. In person, we are able to use our peripheral vision to glance out the window or look at others in the room. On a video call, because we are all sitting in different homes, if we turn to look out the window, we worry it might seem like we're not paying attention. Not to mention that most of us are also staring at a small window of ourselves, making us hyperaware of every wrinkle and expression and how they might be interpreted. Without the visual breaks we need to refocus, our brains grow fatigued.

If this all sounds like bad news, don't despair. We have five research-based tips that can help make video calls less exhausting.

Avoid Multitasking

It's easy to think that you can use the opportunity to do more in less time, but research shows that trying to do multiple things at once cuts into performance. Because you have to turn certain parts of your brain off and on for different types of work, switching between tasks can cost you as much as 40% of your productive time.[1] Researchers at Stanford found that people who multitask can't remember things as well as their more singularly focused peers.[2] The next time you're on a video chat, close any tabs or programs that might distract you (e.g., your inbox or instant messaging), put your phone away, and stay present. We know it's tempting, but try to remind yourself that the message you just got can wait 15 minutes and that you'll be able to craft a better response when you're not also on a video chat.

Build in Breaks

Take mini breaks from video during longer calls by minimizing the window, moving it behind your open applications, or just looking away from your computer for a few seconds. We're all more used to being on video now (and to the stressors that come with nonstop face time). Your colleagues probably understand more than you think—it is possible to listen without staring at the screen for a full 30 minutes. This is an invitation not to start doing something else but to let your eyes rest for a moment. For days when you can't avoid back-to-back calls, consider making meetings 25 or 50 minutes (instead of the standard half hour and hour) to give yourself enough time in between to get up and move around for a bit. If you are on an hour-long video call, make it OK for people to turn off their cameras for parts of the call.

Reduce On-Screen Stimuli

Research shows that when you're on video, you tend to spend the most time gazing at your own face. This can be easily avoided by hiding yourself from view. Still, on-screen distractions go far beyond yourself. You may be surprised to learn that on video, we focus not only on each other's faces but on backgrounds as well. If you're on a call with five people, you may feel like you're in five different rooms at once. You can see their furniture, plants, and wallpaper. You might even strain to see what books they have on their shelves. The brain has to process all of these visual environmental cues at the same time. To combat mental fatigue, encourage people to use plain backgrounds (e.g., a poster of a peaceful beach scene) or agree as a group to have everyone who is not talking turn off their video.

Make Virtual Social Events Opt-In

After a long day of back-to-back video calls, it's normal to feel drained, particularly if you're an introvert. That's why virtual social sessions should be opt-in, meaning whoever owns the event makes it explicit that people are welcome, but not obligated, to join. You might also consider appointing a facilitator if you're expecting a large group. This person can open by asking a question and then make it clear in what order people should speak, so that everyone gets to hear from one another and the group doesn't start talking all at once. It's easy to get overwhelmed if we don't know what's expected of us or if we're constantly trying to figure out when we should or should not chime in.

Switch to Phone Calls or Email

Check your calendar for the next few days to see if there are any conversations you could have over instant message or email. If 4 p.m. rolls around and you're Zoomed-out but have an upcoming one-on-one, ask the person to switch to a phone call or suggest picking up the conversation later so that you can both recharge. Try something like, "I'd love a break from video calls. Do you mind if we do this over the phone?" Most likely the other person will be relieved by the switch, too.

For External Calls, Avoid Defaulting to Video

Many people now feel a tendency to treat video as the default for all communication. In situations where you're communicating with people outside of your organization (clients, vendors, networking, etc.)—conversations for which you used to rely on phone calls—you may feel obligated to send out a video chat link. But a video call is fairly intimate and can even feel invasive in some situations, especially if you don't know each other well. For example, if you're asked to do a career advice call and you don't know the person you're talking to, sticking to phone is often a safer choice. If your client FaceTimes you with no warning, it's OK to decline and suggest a call instead.

Some of these tips might be hard to follow at first (especially that one about resisting the urge to tab-surf during your next Skype call). But taking these steps can help you not feel so exhausted at the thought of another video chat. It's tiring enough trying to adapt to this new normal. Make video calls a little easier for yourself.

Liz Fosslien is an expert on how to help teams and leaders develop the skills that allow them to unlock their full potential. She serves as director of content at Humu, a company that uses nudges to turn strategy into action, and regularly leads sessions related to emotions at work for audiences including TED, LinkedIn, and Google. Liz's work has been featured by *The Economist*, Freakonomics, and NPR.

Mollie West Duffy is an organizational development expert and consultant. She was previously an organizational design lead at global innovation firm IDEO and a research associate for the dean of Harvard Business School, Nitin Nohria, and renowned strategy professor Michael E. Porter. She's written for *Fast Company*, Quartz, *Stanford Social Innovation Review*, *Entrepreneur*, and other digital outlets. Liz and Mollie are the authors of the book *No Hard Feelings: The Secret Power of Embracing Emotions at Work*. Find more from them at www.lizandmollie.com.

NOTES

1. Joshua S. Rubinstein, David E. Meyer, and Jeffrey E. Evans, "Executive Control of Cognitive Processes in Task Switching," *Journal of Experimental Psychology: Human Perception and Performance* 27, no. 4 (August 2001): 763–797, https://www.apa.org/pubs/journals/releases/xhp274763.pdf.

2. Sofie Bates, "A Decade of Data Reveals that Heavy Multitaskers Have Reduced Memory, Stanford Psychologist Says," Stanford News, October 25, 2018, https://news.stanford.edu/2018/10/25/decade-data-reveals-heavy-multitaskers-reduced-memory-psychologist-says/.

SECTION FOUR

Thriving in Virtual Meetings

CHAPTER 14

What Everyone Should Know About Running Virtual Meetings

by Paul Axtell

A big part of the success of remote work is the virtual meeting. It has emerged as the most important method for teams to stay connected, troubleshoot, and discuss any important issues that come up. Yet even though the technology has been steadily improving, we're still stuck in the 1990s when it comes to some outdated practices.

To make sure that your virtual meetings are adding value and velocity to your projects, you need to do three things:

Adapted from content posted on hbr.org, April 14, 2016 (product #H02T9L).

Focus on Relationships

The quality of the relationships among the people in a meeting determines the quality of the conversations that will occur during the meeting. That's why it's important to set aside time to build relationships among team members.

Designate the first part of the meeting to connect and catch up with each other

Make it a practice for the conference lines to be open 10 minutes early. Ask someone to be there to greet and talk with people once the lines are open. If you're leading the meeting, be prepared so that you can spend time chatting rather than answering emails or reviewing your notes. Encourage others to show up early and converse.

Then, at the beginning of each meeting, ask three people to take a couple of minutes to share what's happening with them. These are my favorite prompts to start this brief conversation:

- Please catch us up on one of your projects.

- What's happening in your country?

- How's your family?

During the meeting, use people's names

When you refer to earlier comments, acknowledge the people who said them. Keep a chart next to you so that it's easy to remember who's out there. People love to be recognized, and in virtual meetings, it helps with the sense of community that is diminished by not being in the same space. As a practice, it also pulls meeting participants into a zone of being more attentive and thoughtful.

Prepare, So You Can Be Present and Productive

Publish an agenda

Virtual meetings can be enhanced by having a clear agenda that allows people to understand how the meeting will be conducted. An agenda lets your participants think about and prepare for each topic. This is particularly important for those who speak English as a second language. If people can prepare, they can participate more fully and powerfully. Expecting people to develop their thinking and then express it in the moment, during a meeting, is expecting too much.

The agenda doesn't need to be elaborate. For each topic, answer these questions:

- Why is this topic on our agenda?

- How much time is allocated for this topic?

- Where do we want to be at the end of our discussion?

- What do we need from participants?

Plan on 20% more time than you think you need for each topic

The process of getting broad participation and checking to see if everyone has had a chance to express their views and ask their questions takes time—lots of time. You don't want to feel any pressure to get through an agenda. Clarity and alignment will be sacrificed if you or your team members feel rushed. You can always end early if the time is not needed.

Identify who you want to hear from in each discussion

Ask yourself these questions:

- Who would get the conversation off to a great start?

- Who is most impacted by the topic?

- Who is likely to have different views and ideas?

- Whose experience needs to be brought into the conversation?

Part of feeling included and adding value in a group is being self-expressed—having the opportunity to share what you are thinking about the topic. Being self-expressed can be difficult when you're in the same room, and it's even harder to do virtually. Letting people know that you want broad participation is the first step; calling on people strategically and gently is the second step. Knowing ahead of time who you want to get into the conversation for each topic will make this easy.

Accomplish the Agenda and Get Broad Participation

Review with the group how you intend to manage the conversation

Virtual meetings require a stronger leadership approach, because you don't have access to the nonverbal cues about whether people have questions or would like to get into the conversation. These meetings also require more empathy and thoughtfulness on your part, because people have a sense of being less connected than when they are in the same room.

Ask for the permission you need to be able to relax and enjoy leading the meeting. This is what I usually ask for:

- Permission to be firm about keeping the conversation on track

- Freedom to call on different people when it seems appropriate

- Agreement from everyone about setting aside their technology, unless they have a good reason for keeping it available

I also let people know that while I have a plan for the meeting, I'm very open to their coaching and ideas on making the meeting work for everyone.

Asking for what you want gives you the opportunity to guide the group without making anyone wrong. It also gives the group permission to step outside of their normal ways of interacting and participate authentically. It's easy to be ourselves in small groups of four or five people over coffee. In larger groups and virtual groups, the conversation needs to be set up to be safe and effective.

Consider covering these points in your opening:

With your permission, I intend to manage our conversation today in a deliberate fashion so that we stay on track and make sure everyone gets heard. Please don't interpret this to mean that I intend to be heavy-handed. Just take it to mean I'd like more freedom in keeping the conversation focused and permission to call on people to ensure we have everyone's questions and views expressed before we end a topic.

In each conversation, I'd like to ask certain people to start the topic off. I've made notes on who I think might be impacted and will check with each of you. Of course, if you want to add something and I haven't called on you, please do so. You always have permission to get into any conversation if your ideas, questions, and views have not yet been expressed.

Then, manage the conversation thoughtfully.

Go slowly

Without being able to see people as they speak, it's not only harder to hear, it's more difficult to process what is being said. Speaking succinctly will help, and a calmer pace will provide openings for people to ask their questions. Keep track of who has spoken to help remind you about who you might invite to add to the conversation.

Consider adding a process step to check for clarity on each topic. Without visual clues, you can't always tell when people are not understanding or agreeing. If you have people with different language or cultural backgrounds, getting to clarity and alignment may require more time for going back and forth.

Wrap up each conversation deliberately

Use the five elements of closure, as follows:

- **Check for completion:** Does anyone have anything else to say or ask that has not yet been expressed?

- **Check for alignment:** Is everyone OK with where we ended up in this conversation?

- **Check for next steps:** Are we clear about who will take action and when those actions will be finished?

- **Check for value:** What value are you taking away from this conversation?

- **Check for acknowledgment:** Is there anyone we should acknowledge?

As our work environments continue to move outside the office, it's vital to get virtual meetings right. It is no longer acceptable to sit and multitask to get other work done while you listen in. Of course, the person who calls and leads the meeting is accountable for making it effective. Given the extra difficulty of virtual meetings, we can all make a difference by preparing, asking questions, and sharing our thinking.

———————————

Paul Axtell is an author, speaker, and corporate trainer. He is the author of two award-winning books: *Meetings Matter* and *Ten Powerful Things to Say to Your Kids*, now in its second edition. His most recent books are *Making Virtual Meetings Matter* and *Compassionate Leadership*.

CHAPTER 15

Elevate Your Presence on a Video Call

by Joel Schwartzberg

Videoconferences are becoming more routine for a wide range of business purposes, from staff meetings to brainstorming sessions to major announcements. But communication tactics that work well among colleagues in a conference room may not translate seamlessly to *Brady Bunch*–style quadrants on a computer screen. Organizational behavior professor Andy Molinsky recommends seeing virtual meetings as "an entirely different context, not simply an in-person meeting or a class on a screen."[1]

Adapted from "How to Elevate Your Presence in a Virtual Meeting" on hbr.org, April 8, 2020 (product #H05IOV).

Elevating both your point and your presence in a virtual meeting requires not only engaging in videoconference-friendly tactics but also disabusing yourself of potentially detrimental misconceptions about the medium.

To help you make an impact when your presence is virtual, consider these six recommendations:

Focus on Your Camera, Not Your Colleagues

Every presentation coach will tell you that direct eye contact is a vital way to reinforce your point. In a video-conference, this means looking into the camera, not at the smiling faces of Marcia, Greg, Cindy, Peter, Jan, and Bobby. Speaking into a lens will not feel natural or comfortable—as humans, we're trained to look at the people we're talking to—but remember that entertainers and politicians have been doing it for decades.

While it's challenging to focus on your camera for an entire meeting—especially when others are talking—you increase the impact of your points when you look deep into the dot.

Practice looking into your camera during video-conferences when you speak, even for brief moments. The more you use it, the more comfortable you'll become with it.

Maintain a Strong Voice

I always counsel my students and clients to use a louder-than-usual voice because, in addition to being audible, strong voices convey authority, credibility, and confidence. This concept is just as true in virtual conferences as it is in actual ones. So even though you're using an external or internal microphone and thus may be tempted to speak at a conversational volume, maintain a strong, clear voice, as if you're in a large conference room.

Using a loud voice will also keep you from mumbling or speaking too quickly, due to the amount of breath required.

Frame Yourself Wisely

Proximity plays a big part in how audiences perceive you as a communicator. The farther away or more obscured you appear, the less engaging you will be. In a videoconference, your head and the top of your shoulders should dominate the screen.

If your head is cut off at the top or bottom, you're too close. If your entire torso is in view, you're too far away. If only half of your head is in sight, please adjust the camera.

Also, be mindful of your background. Cluttered rooms make communicators seem disorganized. Distracting elements will pull attention away from you. Find an environment where the background is simple, reflecting your professionalism.

Preparation is critical, so take time before the meeting to pick your location and get your head fully in frame to ensure you're putting your best face forward.

Be Present and Mindful

In a conventional meeting, participants are typically very mindful of their presence. But in a videoconference where you're muted (and maybe in your pajama pants), it's easy to forget you're still being watched. You may be tempted to check your email or attend to other work, but multitasking is perilous, because you don't want to be caught unprepared if asked a question.

Even if you don't need to be fully engaged in the meeting, your professional reputation can suffer if it even looks like you're not paying attention. So close those other windows, turn your phone upside down, and remember that you're always "on camera."

Because you're less aware of social cues in a virtual meeting, it's also important to be mindful of how long and how often you speak, of whether you interrupt other people, and of whether you make a comment that might offend someone present but out of sight. My advice: Don't consider yourself "at home." Consider yourself "at work." Your behavior should follow.

Don't Become Your Own Distraction

In a live meeting, you never have to worry about talking while muted, or annoying ambient noise, or the interference of pets and children. But these are all common pitfalls of virtual meetings, and they can quickly sabotage your point. Your job is to make sure you're remembered for what you did right, not what went wrong, so be mindful of the power you have over both your virtual and physical environments.

Start by training yourself to stay on mute whenever you're not speaking and unmute yourself only when you do speak. Staying on mute shuts out sudden noises as well as routine noises you may not be aware of, like the ticking of a wall clock, the clickety-clack of your typing, or even your own breathing. Unmuting yourself obviously enables you to speak, but—perhaps more important—saves you from being on the receiving end of the embarrassing colleague chorus, "You're on mute!"

Make sure to turn off your camera when you're doing something visually distracting, such as moving to another room or eating. (Drinking is not very distracting, but chewing is another story.)

Finally, if boisterous children or pets want to participate in your call, your colleagues will probably laugh or relate, so don't be worried about or embarrassed by spontaneous distractions. However, if you're tasked with giving a major presentation, try to have someone supervise them in another room, far from the temptation of your presence, or at least create an engrossing activity for them. Parenting and presenting cannot happen simultaneously, and truly important messages require not only your colleagues' full attention but yours as well.

Use the Chat Window as Your Partner

Consider the chat window as not just a discussion platform but a presentational appendage. When you refer to an article or shared document, link to it in the chat. If you run the meeting, link to the agenda. When others are speaking, respond with support or questions. The chat window is a unique opportunity in virtual meetings to elevate your presence, add dimensions to your ideas, and demonstrate that you're fully present.

Whether you've been participating in virtual meetings for years or just started this month, it's important to realize that a videoconference isn't just a discussion over video—it's an entirely new interactive experience, and it requires adapting your perspective, habits, and tactics to make it work effectively for you.

––––––––––

Joel Schwartzberg oversees executive communications for a major national nonprofit, is a professional presentation coach, and is the author of *Get to the Point! Sharpen Your Message and Make Your Words Matter.*

NOTE

1. Andy Molinsky, "Virtual Meetings Don't Have to Be a Bore," hbr.org, March 19, 2020 (product #H05HOO), https://hbr.org/2020/03/virtual-meetings-dont-have-to-be-a-bore.

CHAPTER 16

Break Up Your Brainstorming Sessions

by Liana Kreamer and Steven G. Rogelberg

Remote meetings are plagued with challenges. It's often difficult to find a communication rhythm and flow, especially when there's background noise or poor connection quality. As a result, people may feel detached or removed; they'll engage less, be less present, and multitask more. Voices become lost, especially those of people who tend to be more introverted. These problems are only amplified as meeting size increases, when airtime becomes scarce and anonymity becomes the default.

Adapted from "Break Up Your Big Virtual Meetings" on hbr.org, April 29, 2020 (product #H05L8Y).

To address these issues and gain valuable perspectives from all your meeting attendees, consider modifying your approach. There are two techniques in particular you can try: embracing silence and assigning breakout rooms. While not appropriate for every type of meeting, these tools can be extremely valuable for promoting effectiveness, creativity, engagement, and inclusion.

Embrace Silence to Improve Brainstorming

Research supports the benefits of embracing silence during meetings to better leverage the ideas, perspectives, and insights of all attendees.[1] Silent brainstorming produces significantly more ideas than brainstorming out loud—and these ideas tend to be more creative and of higher quality.

Why? Because encouraging meeting attendees to contribute—silently and individually—allows multiple people to express their ideas all at once. Instead of hearing from one attendee at a time and responding to each person, many voices can be "heard" via this written style of brainstorming. Additionally, because the written brainstorming can be done anonymously, there is less filtering of ideas, which allows attendees to contribute with less fear of judgment.

This technique is particularly beneficial for remote meetings, given the communication and attendee engagement challenges noted above. Here's one way you might execute this technique:

First, when you schedule a remote meeting, review the agenda and highlight the goals of the meeting in the invite. Then, at the start of the meeting itself, share a working document (for example, a Google Doc) with all attendees. The document should contain key questions that need to be answered during the meeting and/or brainstorming prompts.

After explaining that you'll be experimenting with silent brainstorming, encourage all participants to contribute to the document for 10 to 20 minutes, depending on your meeting's needs. During this time, attendees can actively engage in idea generation, responding to one another using commenting functions and collaborating via the document. You'll find that this silent brainstorm will result in an incredibly vibrant exchange of ideas that engages a much larger group of people, with no speaker logjams. As a leader, feel free to chime in, providing direction and asking attendees to elaborate on specific ideas they write about.

Once the brainstorming phase is done, you have several options. If the meeting is relatively small in size (under six attendees), you could debrief with your team—hosting a verbal discussion of what emerged. If the meeting is larger in size, it can end for now. You could then take time to go through the document and see what materialized. You could share general conclusions and next steps with the group in a follow-up email. Or, you might consider sending out a quick survey post-meeting, where folks vote on final options for ways forward or share ratings of prioritization. Separating discussion and deliberation from actual decision making has been found to promote better meeting decision quality.[2]

Use Breakout Rooms to Create a Sense of Accountability

When meetings are large in size (more than six attendees), voices are more at risk of becoming lost. Attendees may miss the opportunity to contribute, feel uncomfortable dominating the discussion, or fear talking over others.

The critical step in making these large meetings better is getting them to feel and function more like small meetings. The easiest way to do this is simple: Break the large group into smaller groups of two or three for a portion of the meeting.

Many video platforms (for example, Zoom, Adobe Connect, and Samba Live) include a "breakout" option, where the leader can assign smaller group discussions within a larger group. The leader can also set a time limit for the breakouts.

Here is an example: Say there are 15 attendees on your team who log on for your weekly staff meeting. You begin this virtual meeting by reviewing meeting goals and objectives with all attendees. This should only take a couple of minutes. Then, you assign breakout chatrooms with three people per room, with the time limit of perhaps 12 minutes. Each subgroup can be charged with a different or similar task.

When time is up, all five breakout groups come back together as a whole. Depending on the assigned task, there are a variety of paths the meeting could take from here: It could end with each subgroup emailing you (the leader) what they came up with. You could then plan next steps. Another path is having one representative from each subgroup report out what they worked on to the wider team while inviting comments and clarification. A final option, depending on the meeting's desired result, is recording the shared recommendations into a poll or form as representatives are presenting them. You could then send a voting link to all group members via the chat function or email to pick which ideas they like best. It should take them no more than a couple of minutes to cast votes. Again, this could be done during or after the meeting.

This breakout strategy allows all attendees to be engaged and involved in developing ideas. More voices are heard with less risk of an attendee flying under the radar. This strategy also creates a sense of accountability, with each group assigned to a specific task. As an added benefit, this technique can save time if a divide-and-conquer approach is used.

If the remote meeting platform you are using does not have a breakout function, there are alternative mechanisms for carrying out this strategy. For example, when you create the subgroups prior to the meeting, ask a representative of each subgroup to create a brief team-meeting invite at a particular time (e.g., 20 minutes prior to the large-group meeting time). After all sub-teams meet to collaborate, the larger group can come together to report ideas and discuss.

Trying out different techniques—whether embracing silence or assigning breakouts—helps mitigate some challenges that virtual meetings face. Importantly, these techniques are not intended to become defaults for all remote meetings. But if you want to hear more ideas from your team, try silent brainstorming. If you have a particularly large team, give breakout rooms a go. After trying out a new technique, reflect and gather feedback from your team on how it went—see what is working and what is not. Learn, reflect, and grow as you expand your meetings toolbox.

Liana Kreamer is a doctoral student at the University of North Carolina at Charlotte, studying organizational science under Dr. Steven G. Rogelberg. She is interested in meeting tactics and cadences, leadership styles, and team dynamics.

Steven G. Rogelberg is the Chancellor's Professor at the University of North Carolina at Charlotte and the author of *The Surprising Science of Meetings: How You Can Lead Your Team to Peak Performance*. He writes and speaks about leadership, teams, meetings, and engagement.

NOTES

1. Steven G. Rogelberg and Liana Kreamer, "The Case for More Silence in Meetings," hbr.org, June 14, 2019. https://hbr.org/2019/06/the-case-for-more-silence-in-meetings.

2. Garold Stasser and William Titus, "Pooling of Unshared Information in Group Decision Making: Biased Information Sampling During Discussion," *Journal of Personality and Social Psychology* 48, no. 6 (1985): 1467–1478. https://psycnet.apa.org/doiLanding?doi=10.1037%2F0022-3514.48.6.1467.

CHAPTER 17

Virtual Off-Sites That Work

by Bob Frisch, Cary Greene, and Dan Prager

Are off-sites off for the foreseeable future? During the pandemic, social distancing recommendations and travel restrictions made it difficult, if not impossible, for many organizations to convene teams of any size within their offices, much less at sessions outside them. Not surprisingly, the initial reaction for most was to postpone or cancel those events, over concern that working together by phone or videoconference wouldn't be as useful or productive as the in-person meeting would have been.

But some of the meaty, controversial types of topics often reserved for the rarefied atmosphere of off-sites

---

Adapted from "Virtual Offsites That Work" on hbr.org, March 25, 2020 (product #H05HZH).

still need to happen. Companies need to learn how to do them virtually, just as they have for other work processes.

The foundation of an effective virtual off-site remains basic meeting management: clear objectives, a well-crafted agenda, concise pre-reads, a well-chosen group of attendees, documented decisions, specific next steps, etc. But with a longer time commitment and a long list of strategic priorities to discuss, it can still seem overwhelming. After all, virtual off-sites were, until the pandemic, a rare exception, and many executives convening or designing these sessions felt they were in uncharted waters. How do you get started?

Drawing from our decades of experience running both in-person and virtual off-sites, we've distilled some practices—over and above the basics—that you can employ to help make yours effective.

Prepare for Your Virtual Off-Site

As with any off-site—in some ways more so with a virtual one—success hinges on what happens before it begins. Here are five steps to take ahead of time:

Provide attendees with the tools they'll need

Whether detailed in the pre-read or in a brief pre-meeting session, instruct everyone on exactly how to install and set up the software and video technology needed to participate. One client even provided a high-definition webcam and an extra monitor to each attendee, which allowed them to see participants on one screen and the shared document on the other.

Ensure everyone knows how to use the technology

Provide opportunities to practice using all the features to be utilized during the off-site. In Zoom, for example, you can set up a test "lobby" so that attendees can familiarize themselves with how to "raise hands" or use the chat function.

Carefully design the off-site's flow, and conduct a dry run

For each section of the meeting, start with what you want to achieve, initially sketch out each exercise independent of the technology, and then consider what's possible with the software. Make sure you keep the activities simple enough for your least technologically advanced attendees. Meeting organizers and facilitators should practice every module of the meeting exactly how it is envisioned. Given technology limitations, it can be more difficult in a virtual setting to shift and redesign a meeting on the fly, so make sure you are equipped with plans B and C if needed.

Assign clear roles

Like a movie production, individuals running the off-site need to be clear on who should do what. Who facilitates each conversation? Who handles the technology, including screen sharing, monitoring chat, and calling on attendees who "raise hands"? Who should attendees contact if they have technical difficulties? Who steps in for the facilitator if he or she encounters technical challenges?

127

When in doubt, limit the size of the group

A common mistake made with off-sites is to invite too many participants. In a virtual setting, with no physical or cost constraints, it is even easier to just send a link to expand the invite list, and before you know it, you're having a town meeting rather than a carefully designed conversation. Use the scope and objectives as a guide to determine who should attend.

Conduct Your Virtual Off-Site

Great off-sites require everyone's full engagement and active participation, which proves even more challenging in a virtual setting. Off-site leaders should consider the following:

Display a welcome screen when people join the meeting

As attendees sign on, welcome them with specific instructions or reminders on the screen to ensure they are set up for the session. For example, in a recent off-site, attendees were greeted with the following message: *Welcome! Please exit full screen (but maximize your viewing window), open your chat window (by clicking on "chat" in the toolbar), and raise your hand (by clicking "raise hand" in the toolbar).*

Make it interactive from the start

We recommend an activity or icebreaker at the beginning to connect participants and make them comfortable with the virtual setting. One client asked each individual to take a minute and share what had been happening in their lives professionally and personally. She went first and modeled the tone and candor of the exercise, explaining that a loved one was ill and describing how it had affected her. Others followed suit, and immediately the group felt more connected and comfortable with each other.

Set clear ground rules

Like any off-site, you need ground rules. Typical ones we use for in-person off-sites still apply—return from breaks on time, be candid and honest, headline your comments, use tricks for cutting people off, etc. Others will be specific to virtual meetings—"raise hand" instead of jumping in, stay on video throughout, mute when possible (but no need to apologize for the occasional barking dog or crying baby).

Take more-frequent breaks

Because participants are sitting in front of a screen for the duration, we find that 15-minute breaks every 90 minutes give people time to reset, handle other business needs, and deal with issues at home. One client has the group take an hourly 60-second "pit stop" together to stretch, do jumping jacks, or take a walk around the living room.

Minimize presentations, maximize discussion

We've said this before, but long presentations can really destroy a meeting's momentum. Background information, whenever possible, should be well edited and provided in advance. If a brief presentation or update is required, use screen sharing to show the material so that everyone can follow along.

Use technology to maximize participation, engagement, and interactivity

Gathering input constantly during a virtual off-site is critical, especially since visual cues are more difficult to read. The features included in videoconferencing software and other easily accessed survey and collaboration tools provide numerous easy-to-use techniques to take everyone's temperature and capture the thinking of meeting attendees, going beyond seeing faces and interpreting body language. And if used correctly, they allow all attendees to more easily put their opinions on the table. Here are a few techniques we've employed during virtual off-sites:

Breakouts

As we learned in chapter 16, putting attendees in small virtual groups helps to break up the day and provides a more intimate setting to solve problems. One client was amazed when—with the push of a button—20 meeting attendees suddenly found themselves each transported into five-person videoconferences, with our facilitators dropping in and out of their conversations. After 20 minutes of drafting their approach to a problem and writing it up on a PowerPoint slide, they were brought back to the larger group. While breakouts need to be planned well (we find filling out a common template to be a great addition), they can be as much a part of a virtual off-site as a traditional one.

Voting

Poll people early and often. Technology embedded in most videoconference systems or phone-based tools such as Poll Everywhere allow participants to respond anonymously to questions in real time. Remember, don't just ask yes-or-no questions. Questions that ask attendees to indicate the extent to which they agree with a statement, on a 1-to-5 scale, often go further in teasing out opinions virtually.

Stamping

Similar to placing dots on a wall chart in an in-person off-site, allowing participants to annotate or "stamp" a shared screen is a powerful way for all attendees to provide feedback, indicate preferences, or identify where they have questions. In a recent off-site, a client shared a slide containing 20 potential products and asked each attendee to place a stamp (a star in this case) on the five the organization should pursue over the next 12 months. Very quickly, it was apparent where the group was aligned and where opinions differed.

Chat

Most videoconferencing technologies offer a chat function. While you might need some ground rules to prevent the conversation from becoming unruly, chat provides an additional forum for attendees to offer opinions to the full group or directly to the meeting facilitators. For instance, as part of one exercise, we asked attendees to submit new growth ideas to the full group via chat, which allowed us to more efficiently develop a consolidated list to review with the group.

Gather session feedback

Solicit attendees' feedback while the experience is fresh in their minds. Going back to the very beginning of the meeting—from the moment they received the invitation through the pre-meeting survey, the pre-read, the agenda, the technology, the discussion—ask them questions like: What could be improved? If we could "run the tape" over, what would be different? Then ask: What went well? What should be repeated? What did you like?

It's impossible to replicate the experience of an in-person off-site in an online setting. But with the right preparation, a focus on good meeting practices, careful use of various tools, some rehearsal, and a willingness to experiment as a team, it's not only feasible but relatively easy to conduct virtual off-sites that allow you and your team to productively tackle even the toughest issues. And it's likely you may have to do just that for quite some time.

—————

Bob Frisch is the managing partner of the Strategic Off-sites Group. He is the author or coauthor of four *Harvard Business Review* articles, including "Off-Sites That Work" (June 2006) and "When Teams Can't Decide"

(November 2008), in addition to numerous articles for hbr.org. Bob is also the author of *Who's in the Room?* and coauthor of *Simple Sabotage.*

Cary Greene is a partner of the Strategic Offsites Group. An expert in strategic alignment and facilitation, he is a trusted adviser to leaders of public, private, and family-owned organizations. Cary is coauthor of *Simple Sabotage*, the *Harvard Business Review* article "Leadership Summits That Work" (March 2015), and over 10 articles for hbr.org.

Dan Prager is a senior manager at the Strategic Offsites Group, a Boston-based consulting firm focused on designing and managing strategic conversations for executive teams, directors, and boards of some of the world's leading organizations.

CHAPTER 18

Stop Zoning Out in Zoom Meetings

by Sarah Gershman

You join a videoconference call. You're one of nine faces on the screen. About 10 minutes in, your mind starts to wander and you realize you have no idea what the last person just said. You pretend to keep listening while also checking your inbox. By the end of the meeting, you've caught up on some email but ultimately feel like it was another waste of time. For many of us, this scenario sounds all too familiar.

There is a lot of sound advice about how leaders can run more effective virtual meetings. While this advice is critical, what is often overlooked is the role that *listeners* play in ensuring a meeting's success.

Adapted from content posted on hbr.org, May 4, 2020 (product #H05L11).

In 1913, Max Ringelmann, a French architectural engineer, made a discovery that explains why virtual meetings are often so unsuccessful. Ringelmann asked a team of people to pull on a rope. He then asked individuals—separately—to pull on the same rope. He noticed that when people worked as individuals, they put more effort into pulling than when they worked as a team. We call this the "Ringelmann effect." The bigger the group, the less responsibility each individual feels to ensure success. If one does not feel critical to a mission's success, it's easy to tune out or put in less effort. No one will notice anyway, right?

In virtual meetings—and especially on conference calls—the Ringelmann effect is magnified. When you are not in the room to help "pull the rope" for a meeting, you might feel less motivated to listen and participate. The less you feel needed, the more distracted you will become, and the less you will give to the meeting. And the less you give, the less fulfilling the experience.

Unfortunately, this dynamic of distraction not only makes for poor meeting outcomes, it also makes for a miserable experience for you, the listener. A study by psychologists at Harvard University showed that distraction from the present increases unhappiness.[1] While it may be easy and tempting to get distracted during meetings, it's ultimately unfulfilling.

How can you minimize the Ringelmann effect and give more to (and get more from) virtual meetings? It's not through more or louder participation. Rather, the secret to effective participation involves thoughtful and targeted *listening*. Especially in a virtual context, listening needs to be active, participatory, and helpful. Here are five strategies to listen more effectively in your next virtual meeting:

Define Your Value Beforehand

Take a few moments before the meeting starts to distill the purpose of the meeting and what your value could be. What is the most critical information you have? What is it you want to contribute? Be ready with those points. If you do not have a critical role to play or do not need to present any information, identify exactly what you hope to learn from the call. Figuring this out beforehand will help you listen more carefully to what's being said and strengthen a listening muscle for future meetings.

Acknowledge Previous Statements

Participants sometimes jump in to make their point without first listening to or acknowledging what has just been said. In response, people may repeat or rehash earlier points, as they do not feel heard or understood. All of this slows down the meeting and leads to a disjointed and frustrating conversation. This dynamic is magnified in a virtual meeting, where people often talk over each other. Active listening can help. Before you raise a new topic, reiterate what you just heard or the previous point you plan to riff on—even ask the speaker whether you've characterized their point correctly. Not only does this help the conversation, it also makes it more likely that others will hear what you have to say. People are more likely to listen if they first feel heard.

Connect the Dots

Leading a virtual meeting is hard. Participants often provide scattershot commentary, and it's tough for a leader to keep the conversation running smoothly. Again, your ability to listen will help. Listen carefully to participants' contributions, and then see how you can reflect on what you've heard to help move the conversation forward. For example, let's say over the course of a meeting you notice that several participants mention that a client is frustrated. You might say, "I've heard several people say that the client seems frustrated. Does anyone have any thoughts on why this frustration is happening right now?" Notice that you are not actually giving any new information. By listening first and then connecting the dots, you can help the other participants understand the larger dynamic and guide the conversation in a productive direction. Effective listening manifests itself when you speak up and reflect on what you've heard.

Bring Your Attention Back

Despite your best efforts to listen, it's natural for your mind to wander during the call. It happens to even the best listeners. As with meditation, try to gently note the distracting thought and return your attention to the call. It helps to have a pad of paper next to you. This act of writing down wandering thoughts allows you to put the thought somewhere so that you can return to it later, after the meeting has ended. You can also write down any distracting thoughts before the meeting starts, which can help you to be more present and ready to listen.

Don't Be Afraid to Ask a Question

Sometimes when you get distracted and then return your focus to the meeting, you may find that you are lost, as the conversation has moved in a new direction and you missed the transition. Give yourself a few minutes to get back on track, and don't be afraid to ask a clarifying question. You might say, "I apologize. I lost track of the conversation for a moment. Would someone please help me understand why we are now focusing on . . ." This may also help others on the call, as it is likely you are not the only one who is confused.

In the isolation of the virtual world, we often feel like we have to fight to be heard, lest our voice get lost in the noise. Once again, listening comes to the rescue. Ironically, one of the best ways to be heard is to be a good listener. Thoughtful, active listening raises your status in the conversation and makes it more likely that others will want to sit up and listen to you. Perhaps most important, active, thoughtful listening is a precious gift, providing meaningful connection with your colleagues.

Sarah Gershman is president of Green Room Speakers, a communications firm based in Washington, DC. She is a professor at the McDonough School of Business at Georgetown University, where she teaches public speaking to students from around the globe.

NOTE

1. Steve Bradt, "Wandering Mind Not a Happy Mind," *Harvard Gazette*, November 11, 2010, https://news.harvard.edu/gazette/story/2010/11/wandering-mind-not-a-happy-mind/.

Being the Boss

CHAPTER 19

How to Manage Remote Direct Reports

by Rebecca Knight

Geographically dispersed teams are increasingly common in the modern workplace. Perhaps you're based in your company's New York headquarters, your team works in Los Angeles, and you also manage a group of developers in Minsk. Or maybe your entire team works remotely. How do you overcome the challenges of supervising employees in different locations and time zones? What steps should you take to build trust and open lines of communication? How should you establish routines?

Adapted from content posted on hbr.org, February 10, 2015 (product #H01VI9).

And how do you help remote workers feel part of a team?

What the Experts Say

One of the biggest misconceptions about managing remote workers is that it requires an entirely different skill set. "We have a tendency to overcompensate and approach remote workers and virtual teams as these mythical beasts," says Mark Mortensen, an associate professor of organizational behavior at INSEAD. "But you shouldn't think about them in a fundamentally different way. They are still people working in an organization to get stuff done. Treat them as such." That said, managers must put in extra effort to cultivate a positive team dynamic and ensure remote workers feel connected to other colleagues. It requires a "proactive approach," says Keith Ferrazzi, the founder and chair of Ferrazzi Greenlight. So, whether your team is composed of people in far-flung locations in distant time zones or employees who work from home (or a combination of both), here are some pointers to keep things running smoothly.

Set expectations

"As the manager, you need to set clear, deliberate expectations in advance and establish ground rules for how interactions will take place," says Ferrazzi. If you fail to do this, "things will break down immediately." He recommends "establishing clear lines of accountability" from the outset of the working relationship by setting monthly, quarterly, and yearly performance goals as well as "targets for what 'hitting it out of the park' would mean." Then, just as you would with employees working down the hall, "you should check in regularly on progress" through an agreed-upon schedule. Mortensen adds: Be sure to make it clear that you're "applying the same metrics to the rest of the team." Remote workers "need to know that they're not being treated differently and there's no inequity."

Visit on a predictable schedule

There are no rules governing precisely how often you need to see your remote workers in person, but Mortensen recommends visiting them regularly if possible, especially in the early stages. "If you can get yourself to their location when you first start working together, that's invaluable," he says. "Seeing people one-on-one, face-to-face, sets the tone and gives people a sense of comfort." As the arrangement stabilizes, "predictability is more important than a particular frequency," he says. "If your direct report knows you're there every six months, it helps build trust." When you're at their location, make an effort to "understand their environment and get a sense of what it's like" to work from afar. "Join in on a conference call to the home office so you can get a glimpse of [the situation] from their perspective," Mortensen says.

Encourage communication

The key to managing relationships with remote employees, says Ferrazzi, is to "set an appropriate cadence" of communications—including how quickly employees need to respond to email; what follow-up steps should be taken; and on which days check-in calls should occur.

"If you, the manager, don't create good, open communication channels, the remote worker will feel, well, 'remote' and forgotten," he says. Encourage the use of instant messaging, blogs, wikis, and other online collaboration tools and apps. Your team must "understand that they have an obligation" to stay in regular contact, says Mortensen.

Spark impromptu interactions

Unplanned conversations between coworkers are "important for flows of knowledge throughout an organization," says Mortensen, which is why you—the manager—have a responsibility to "literally create watercooler moments" in a virtual setting. Video links between offices "create a shared space and provide more opportunities for these spontaneous but often very productive" workplace conversations, he says. "It might feel weird the first day it's on, but by the 10th day, people are more comfortable." When it's not possible (or preferable) to have a camera that's always on, Ferrazzi recommends regular use of technologies like Skype and WebEx. Video technology, he says, "brings us together and connects us, increasing the intimacy of our relationships with one another."

Nurture familiarity

Building trust and familiarity with your direct reports requires that you get to know them on a personal level. With remote workers "this takes additional effort," says Mortensen. He suggests reserving the first few minutes of calls and videoconferences to simply "chew the fat." You should talk about "the things you usually talk about at work"—weekend plans, kids, pets, or last night's big game. Encourage your direct reports to do the same with their remote colleagues. This social bonding "builds essential empathy, trust, and camaraderie," Ferrazzi says. "What binds together virtual teams are the personal details."

Make them feel part of the team

Physical distance can sometimes create an "us versus them" feeling. Mortensen says it's critical that you "watch the language you use when talking about remote workers and make sure you're not creating fractures within your team." Concentrate on what you and your direct reports have in common—organizational goals and objectives, for example. Remember, too, remote team members often feel that they're somewhat invisible and "that their actions and efforts aren't noticed." Being generous with public praise and acknowledging remote employees helps "make sure their work is recognized" and is a signal to "coworkers that they're pulling their weight," says Mortensen.

Principles to Remember

Do:

- Get to know your remote reports on a personal level by reserving a few minutes during meetings and calls for casual workplace conversations

- Establish a schedule of communication both between you and your remote employee and between the remote employee and the rest of the team

- Use video technology to spark spontaneous inter-actions among your team members

Don't:
- Evaluate the job performance of remote work-ers differently from the way you assess colocated colleagues; instead, apply the same metrics across your team

- Worry too much about setting up constant in-person meetings with your remote workers; predict-able visits are more important than frequent ones

- Forget to acknowledge the work of remote workers so that their efforts don't go unnoticed

Case Study #1: Unite Employees Around a Common Goal

Arvind Sarin, the cofounder and CEO of Copper Mobile, a mobile app development firm, manages more than 100 employees split between the company's headquar-ters in Dallas, Texas, and its office in Noida, India. The majority of the company's clients are in North America. Because of the difference in time zones, there was some resentment between team members. "There was still a feeling of: 'Oh, that team over there rolls out at 6 p.m. while we're here working late into the night,'" he explains.

To mitigate the building resentment and bring the team together, Arvind decided to be more open about the company's overarching goals and financial targets. He took a new approach with a big project Copper Mo-bile was working on for a Los Angeles–based dating company. "In order to get everyone on the same page, I painted a picture of our strategy so that everyone—from developers in India to the leadership team here—would know what we're doing," he says.

His aim was to "lay it all out" for employees in both offices "so that everyone knew what to expect" and felt bonded by a common goal—to successfully execute the project. In a series of meetings, "we explained how much revenue this client would bring in, what the billing rates would be, how long we expected the engagement to last, what the workflow would be like, and how we viewed this customer as a strategic client."

Arvind's transparency about the project united the team and motivated employees to work together. The project was a big success. "When you don't give people information, they assume the worst," he says. "Restating our vision and reminding people of what we were trying to achieve helped a lot."

Case Study #2: Seize Opportunities for In-Person Team Bonding

Manon DeFelice, the founder and CEO of Inkwell, a specialized professional staffing company, manages an entirely virtual team.

At the moment, she has 11 employees—all of whom work from home—spread across the U.S. Recruiting and business development are run out of New York; legal is in Washington, DC; and she also has colleagues in Austin, Miami, and Minneapolis. Manon herself is based in Connecticut. "Because we're a virtual team, we don't have that daily office chitchat," she says, adding that she has to work hard to make sure she is close to her colleagues and that everyone on her team "feels connected to, and trusts, each other."

To encourage bonding, Manon tries to seize every opportunity to gather the group together face-to-face. She recently had a big pitch meeting in New York City. Instead of enlisting the help of only local employees, she invited everyone on the team to the city and then took them all out for a celebratory dinner. "We are not renting expensive office space so I like to spend money taking my team out to nice restaurants. I want people to get to know each other—to talk to each other about their kids and their spouses—just as they would if they worked in an office together."

Another way Manon lifts team morale is by being generous with praise. She regularly sends companywide emails praising the team and singling out colleagues for a job well done. The emails, she says, provide public validation. "In an office, your boss might call to you from down the hall and say: 'Awesome job on that project!' and your colleagues would hear that and know you're working hard." Remote workers, though, don't have that happen. "So I do public thank-you emails, and cc others as a way for them to 'eavesdrop' on the conversation."

––––––––––

Rebecca Knight is a freelance journalist in Boston and a lecturer at Wesleyan University. Her work has been published in the *New York Times*, *USA Today*, and the *Financial Times*.

CHAPTER 20

5 Questions (Newly) Virtual Leaders Should Ask Themselves

by Melissa Raffoni

For some people, working from home and communicating through digital mediums like Slack, Zoom, and WebEx has been the norm for years. Many business models have long supported virtual work as a necessity to accommodate employees and clients in various locations. Still, while technology has improved our ability to get work done and communicate remotely, managers

---

Adapted from "5 Questions That (Newly) Virtual Leaders Should Ask Themselves" on hbr.org, May 1, 2020 (product #H05L1W).

haven't always had a set of best practices for leading re-mote teams at a high capacity.

My intent here is to challenge leaders to pause and identify what they need to do differently to not only sus-tain but also strengthen their skills in a virtual setting.

First, it's important to be aware of the factors that make working together virtually such a challenge:

- **For some, it's uncomfortable.** Every day, I watch my teenagers laugh and chat with their friends on FaceTime, as if they were just another person in the room. But for many of us adults who didn't grow up with that same technology, it can still be quite uncomfortable. This lack of comfort makes it harder for some to open up, connect, trust, and communicate with each other virtually. If you are a leader in a virtual setting, you may be struggling to display the same level of authenticity and provide your team with the same sense of safety as you did in person.

- **Interpersonal dynamics are harder to manage.** Both for technical reasons and because people are harder to read over video, the appropriate affect, tone, pacing, and facial expressions that we rely on for effective communication in person are more difficult to give and receive virtually, especially in group settings.

- **You can easily lose people's attention.** It's chal-lenging enough to engage people in face-to-face meetings, but virtual meetings often come with a plethora of new distractions that you have little control over.

- **New skills are required from you.** Whether it's managing tech, maintaining strong facilitation skills, or rethinking agendas, virtual is different from in-person. Knowing that is half the battle.

With these factors as a backdrop, ask yourself five questions to ensure you are being the best leader you can be as you manage your team from home.

Am I being strategic enough?

Strong leaders practice strategic communications in every interaction, be it a full-day meeting, an hour-long meeting, a sales call, a one-on-one check-in, or even an email. But communicating virtually requires even more strategic planning because you can't rely as much on human connection or charisma to carry you. Before every exchange, take time to think about your purpose, audience, and the context of the exchange. Then write down your objectives, agenda, and the amount of time you want to spend on each item.

It helps to make your objectives broader than usual. For example, what do you want the other person (or people) to feel after you talk? Challenge yourself to up the engagement quotient to make up for the deficit of face-to-face interaction. This means asking more questions during your interactions, checking in with team members to make sure you are aligned, and leaving extra time for those moments to take place during presentations or group meetings.

Have I revamped communication plans for my direct team and the organization at large?

Revisit and potentially revamp your communication protocols with direct reports, employees, board members, and any other audiences you regularly work with, especially as more of your operations become virtual. For example, think about how you will run your weekly check-ins with team members. Will you hold these meetings by phone, over Slack, or through a scheduled video call? While best practice says video is best, you may need to adjust your approach based on the preferences of individual employees. The same goes for meetings with clients and other stakeholders.

Using a table in a Word document or Google Sheet can help you create a comprehensive plan for different types of meetings. Create at least four columns, including one for each of the below items:

- Mode of communication (e.g., video, phone, Slack)

- Meeting cadence (e.g., weekly, monthly)

- Meeting agenda (e.g., team building, check-ins)

- Meeting participants (e.g., managers, board members)

Fill out your table based on how you worked prior to becoming virtual, then revamp the entire plan to adjust to your situation.

As you begin to revamp, challenge everything you considered best practice before, from the size of your meetings to the time allotted. Ask: Should a video call be used for all announcements, or can I simply write a status report to update the team? Do I need to schedule more check-ins with my direct reports to make up for the lack of being in-person? Does that meeting that took an hour in the office need to last the full 60 minutes online? Should each communication be followed by a detailed email summary to keep everyone on the same page?

Looking at the entire plan will allow you to optimize it.

How might I reset roles and responsibilities to help people to succeed?

Some people thrive when working remotely, while others may feel a lack of motivation or encounter other unforeseen challenges. Though it may not always be apparent who is struggling, as a leader, it's your job to check in regularly with team members about how they are coping. During your one-on-ones, ask, "How are things going for you? What challenges are you facing? What do you think you need to be successful? How can I, or the team, help?"

Through these discussions, reevaluate each person's strengths and weaknesses. You may find that you need to shift responsibilities around or invest in training sessions for those who feel less comfortable. For example, one of your team members might excel at running meetings in person but lack either the technical or facilitation skills to run them remotely. Or you may find that you have an individual who participates actively during in-person meetings but not as actively in virtual ones.

Because change—like shifting a role and taking on new work—can bring up sensitivities in people, it's important to frame any suggestions you make as opportunities for growth. By diagnosing your direct report's strongest and weakest points, placing them where they can succeed, and providing them with guidance when they are struggling, you will not only help your team be more productive, you will help your employees develop. In these conversations, be sure to ask for their feedback and thoughts with respect to how the team can improve. Remember that respect, authenticity, and caring are foundational to strong leadership.

Am I keeping my eye on (and communicating about) the big picture?

When you're working remotely, it's easy to focus solely on the tactical—to stay glued to your computer, fielding email after email, in an earnest, unorganized fashion. With your to-do list looming in front of you, and no colleagues to pull you out of your head, you may be tempted to stay buried in the weeds. But people rely on leaders for direction. This means, no matter how many small tasks are clogging your calendar, you need to be able to pick your head up and keep one eye on the bigger picture.

Be sure to carve out time to work *on* the business (strategy), as opposed to working *in* the business (operations). Do this by blocking off time on your personal calendar to think about strategy. Or, if your thoughts are clear, schedule a strategy session with your team. Use this time to revisit fundamental questions about the business and organization, like: Is our value proposition clear to our customers? Are there opportunities for us to improve our business model? Is our team engaged, productive, and inspired to do their best work?

What more can I do to strengthen our company culture?

I am continually struck by the stories I hear of teams that grew even stronger during the Covid-19 pandemic, despite the new work-from-home situations, stress, and anxieties that they also dealt with. Many of the most resilient leaders I work with accomplished this by finding opportunities to align, engage, and inspire their teams around a purpose.

Regularly set aside time for team members to highlight and share wins delivered to customers, each other, or to the business itself. If well-crafted, you can tie the "bright spot" sharing to the company's vision, mission, or values, reiterating the importance of the organization's purpose and the essential role that everyone plays in achieving it. If meeting time is tight, a quick email or another type of nonverbal communication can also be used.

To bring people together, you may also consider prioritizing some team-building avenues that were less essential before. Many of our clients have begun conducting virtual social hours, meditation groups, art-sharing clubs, team music performances, and fitness challenges. While these options may not be for everyone, they are just a handful of examples we have seen initiate positive team dynamics. Even something as simple as starting a meeting by asking people to bring a video, a meme, or a photo that gives them joy can foster camaraderie and a needed laugh.

The skills you build as a virtual leader will continue to serve you well into the future. New opportunities will open up—maybe full virtual workforces on a level we've never seen. And thanks to the experience you're getting through your own remote work, you'll be ready for it, with new skills in place to truly lead—whether from home or the office—more effectively than before.

————————

Melissa Raffoni is CEO of The Raffoni Group, a boutique professional services firm that helps CEOs realize their highest ambitions while improving the quality of their personal and professional lives. She is recognized for her thought leadership in the areas of CEO effectiveness, strategy, execution, leadership, and organizational alignment.

CHAPTER 21

Make Yourself Available to Remote Employees

by Sabina Nawaz

In the global transition from corporate hallways to home offices, we've left something behind: meaningful access to managers. Gone are the instant answers to unblock progress, information streams that managers are privy to before the rest of the organization, informal feedback and coaching while walking together after a meeting, and predictable processes and structures for communicating about work and ensuring mutual accountability.

One of my coaching clients, a senior director, started working remotely during the pandemic and struggled

---

Adapted from "How Managers Can Support Remote Employees" on hbr.org, April 1, 2020 (product #H05ICU).

with the transition. During a coaching call, he lamented, "I'm stalled because I don't know how to connect with my manager on the less-formal stuff—the way I used to." He's not alone. The physical absence of a manager is frustrating employees and stalling work.

But managers find themselves struggling too. For every employee who is trying to reach their manager, a manager is attempting to connect with half a dozen or more direct reports, plus trying to get direction from their own boss. In a poll of my coaching clients about their biggest challenges while working remotely, the key themes were about how to stay connected with each team member, help manage their own and others' stress, maintain team morale and motivation, run engaged meetings, track and communicate progress, and help their team shed nonessential work.

My clients—managers in a variety of organizations—and I have worked through several scenarios and arrived at six strategies to augment availability to employees when working remotely. We're seeing indications that implementing these strategies can reduce manager and employee stress, address concerns about employee work progress, increase productivity for them and their teams, and restore and maintain healthy communication channels.

Bridge Distance Through Frequent Connections

Yuval (names have been changed), the CEO of a 1,000-person high-tech company, messages or calls his direct reports at least once a day, usually without a specific agenda. He says things like, "Checking to see if you need anything from me," "What questions do you have for me today?," "Just learned about X and want you to be the first to know," and "Thinking of you; reminded of our winter team outing and your killer s'mores as I look at the picture on my home-office wall." Instead of simply asking his direct reports to get in touch with him as needed, Yuval proactively manages the frequency of connection. This way, he always has a finger on the pulse of his team, especially those directs hesitant to reach out and add more to their boss's plate.

Blast Through Questions with Office Hours

Managers make dozens of decisions daily and provide their people with scores of data points via informal conversations. These interactions don't merit full meetings, but when they're ignored, little things can languish and become looming problems. Marissa, executive director of a nonprofit, has started holding office hours: an hour a day in which she invites her direct reports to join her on a videoconferencing app if they have concerns that can be addressed in 10 minutes or less. When one person joins, she locks the meeting—the online version of shutting the office door. Everyone understands they should try back in about 10 minutes if a lock is in place. For more-complex issues, Marissa asks her employees to schedule a dedicated meeting. Allocating time to deal with the flurry of daily issues maintains work fluidity and prevents small sore spots from festering into large pain points.

Provide Stability Through Consistent Rituals

In lives riddled with unpredictability and constant change, rituals provide predictability and structure. While we don't know what challenges we'll face tomorrow, we do know there will be some. We can better manage the unpredictable by containing it within structured rituals whenever feasible. Here are some examples of how managers have ritualized their availability: 15-minute morning check-ins to regroup on overnight developments and establish a course for the day; opening a meeting by having everyone share one word to describe their current state of mind followed by an elaborative sentence (or saying "pass"); or a theme for each week's meeting, such as everyone wears a hat. By creating a predictable ritual and leading by example, managers can foster a sense of connection, safety, and fun, even while their teams are buffeted by the forces of change.

Enhance Safety Through Clear Boundaries

Expanding your availability as a manager can also have downsides. Some team members might not desire frequent connection all the time. Others might want more time from you than your capacity allows. Be transparent about your availability plan, then set boundaries and invite others to do the same. You can say, for example, "I'm prioritizing my time with you. I'll reach out in a variety of ways, from checking in with you daily to having office hours. Let me know if you need some space and don't want to connect quite so frequently. I'll also do my best to respond to your messages the same day. However, I'm reserving 30 minutes each day at noon to have lunch with my family and will not be available." By setting expectations and giving others space, we meet people where they are and give them permission to set their own boundaries.

Stay Ahead of the Game by Inviting Problems, Not Just Solutions

When you're the boss, being out of the loop should worry you. So invite your team to come to you with problems, even if they don't yet have solutions. Consider saying, "It's hard to stay on top of everything when we're all remote. If you see signs of trouble, issues that aren't visible to me, don't wait to come to me until you have an accompanying solution. Bring me your early indicators, and together we'll devise experiments to tackle the challenge." Explicitly signaling you want to know about budding problems will enable greater periscopic vision and access to broader sets of solutions.

Enable Capacity Through Feedback

The subtleties of nonverbal communication are lost in remote work, even with the video turned on. Reserve time at the end of each day to provide specific positive feedback for good work (not just great work). Appreciation expressed can help smooth a lot of disruptive discomforts. Also provide timely corrective feedback before shortfalls aggravate your pile of problems. Small and frequent performance guidance circumvents major corrections down the road and allows everyone to stay in sync despite distance and daily change.

Researchers Teresa Amabile and Steven Kramer have extensively studied employee motivation and found that making progress in meaningful work is the key to keeping employees engaged. While remote work can cause stress and add many complications to daily activities, your job as a manager is to remove as many barriers to forward momentum as possible. By communicating a clear availability plan, you can help your team members feel better connected to you and address any concerns or questions as they arise.

Sabina Nawaz is a global CEO coach, leadership keynote speaker, and writer working in more than 26 countries. She advises C-level executives in *Fortune* 500 corporations, government agencies, nonprofits, and academic organizations. Sabina has spoken at hundreds of seminars, events, and conferences, including TEDx, and has written for FastCompany.com, Inc.com, and Forbes.com, in addition to hbr.org.

CHAPTER 22

How to Keep Your Team Motivated, Remotely

by Lindsay McGregor and Neel Doshi

Many leaders establish the foundations for remote work: ensuring colleagues have set up their tech tools, defined their processes, and permanently logged in to their videoconference accounts. But this is just the first step toward creating an effective work environment for remote employees. The next critical question is: How do you motivate people who work from home?

It's often easy for remote employees to focus more on tactical work—answering the right number of tickets,

Adapted from content posted on hbr.org, April 9, 2020 (product #H05JQI).

or following the approved project plan—rather than adapting to solve the bigger, newer problems the business may be facing.

But some teams rise above the rest, regardless of the challenges. They win market share. They earn lifelong customer love. They keep their productivity high, or higher. In other words, they adapt. Though the academic research on remote productivity is mixed, with some saying it declines while others promise it increases, our research suggests that your success will depend on how you do it.

Between 2010 and 2015, we surveyed more than 20,000 workers around the world, analyzed more than 50 major companies, and conducted scores of experiments to figure out what motivates people, including how much working from home plays into the equation. When we measured the total motivation of people who worked from home versus the office, we found that working from home was less motivating. Even worse, when people had no *choice* in where they worked, the differences were enormous. Total motivation dropped 17 points, the equivalent of moving from one of the best to one of the most miserable cultures in their industries.

We identified three negative motivators that often lead to reduced work performance—and these likely spiked during the coronavirus pandemic. *Emotional pressure* and *economic pressure* soar as people worry about losing their jobs, paying their rent, and protecting their health. The barrage of news, questions on how to safely get groceries, and fears for relatives are deeply distressing. *Inertia* for work is bound to increase as people wonder if there's a point in even trying.

We also identified three positive motivators that often lead to increased work performance. *Play*, the motive that most boosts performance, can decrease if it is harder for people to get things done from home. For example, people may miss the joy of problem-solving with a colleague, or the ease of making a decision when everyone is in one room. *Purpose* could also decline with a team's decreasing visibility into their impact on clients or colleagues, especially if no one is there to remind them. Lastly, *potential* could decline if people can't gain access to colleagues who teach and develop them.

If business leaders don't move to change this, shifts in people's motivation will ultimately lead to a decline in adaptability, quality, and creativity.

What Can Business Leaders Do?

When a colleague of ours was diagnosed with cancer, our first instinct was to reduce her work so she could focus on her illness. To be sure, there were times she needed 100% rest. But we quickly realized that we had taken away a major source of her play and purpose. Her work was a much-needed break from the anxiety-inducing news she received each day.

This was also true for the firms we worked with during the financial crisis. We found that analysts trying to shore up the markets had the highest motivation levels of their careers during 18-hour workdays. Military veterans we interviewed talked about their highest-stakes days in the same way. Similarly, during the early days of the pandemic, many citizens organized volunteer bike courier clubs. Fitness instructors led classes from their rooftops or streamed them for free online.

It's important for leaders to follow suit and remember that work can deliver a much-needed boost to their teams, even when there's little choice involved in their work-from-home situation. The key is to resist the temptation to make work tactical only through strict processes, rules, and procedures. While some degree of boundaries and guidelines help people move quickly, too many create a vicious spiral of demotivation. In such cases, people tend to stop problem-solving and thinking creatively, and instead do the bare minimum.

If you want your teams to be engaged in their work, you have to make their work engaging. The most powerful way to do this is to give people the opportunity to experiment and solve problems that really matter. These problems won't be the same for every team or organization. They may not even be easy to identify at first. Your employees will need your help to do this. Ask them: *Where can we deliver amazing service to our customers? What's broken that our team can fix? What will drive growth? Why are these problems critical, valuable, and interesting?*

Today, we're collaborating with teams across the globe that are seizing this way of working. A pharmaceutical company's clinical trials team is experimenting with ways they can help hospitals prioritize trials and maintain safety. Teams across the tech unicorn Flexport are generating ideas on how to ship critical goods around the world, keep their clients' supply chains running, and share tips to keep their suppliers in business. An insurance company is testing ways to prioritize their skyrocketing internal chat volumes and process claims in timely ways. In the teams we work with, we've seen productivity remain high, and in some cases improve.

What has made them so successful is that they are not relying solely on giant new programs or approaches that need CEO approval. They are simply finding ways to make sure every single person on their teams feels like they have a challenge that they can help solve. In your own cases, this challenge can range from something as small as how to better greet customers or accommodate new schedules to something as big as moving your previously in-person business online.

Taking This Back to Your Teams

This all may sound great in theory, but if you're wondering how to start, you're not alone. Few organizations have been taught how to identify when and where it is OK to experiment with new ways of working—despite the fact that experimentation results in a 45-point increase in employee motivation.

There's a simple set of recommendations we give to teams who are working remotely.

First, what you measure is the single strongest signal to your people of what you care about. Measure your team's total motivation using a survey tool. Then, have a discussion with them about what might be driving their motivation up or down and what would be helpful to maximize their motivation and experimentation in the weeks to come.

You might ask questions like: *How are your circumstances affecting you at the moment? What tips do you have for how to motivate yourself and find play and purpose?* This is your time to listen and create a safe environment in which everyone can talk.

Second, make sure your weekly routines are not focused only on the tactical work—the concrete plans you need to execute, like the tickets you need to answer or boxes you need to check. Much of your week should also be focused on adaptive performance, where there is no plan to follow but instead experimentation and problem-solving.

Generally, we recommend a simple rhythm for remote teams:

Monday: Hold a performance-cycle meeting for the team that covers the following.

1. What impact did we have last week, and what did we learn?

2. What commitments do we have this week? Who is on point for each?

3. How can we help each other with this week's commitments?

4. What are the areas where we should experiment to improve performance this week?

5. What experiments will we run, and who is on point for each?

Tuesday–Thursday: Have at least one individual meeting with each of your team members. To help motivate your employees, focus on helping them tackle challenges that are a slight stretch. You can also coordinate small group meetings in which employees can collaborate on the week's experiments and tackle problems together.

Friday: Focus on reflection. Showcase and gather input on the experiments of the week. This might include presentations from project groups during which team members share metrics and insights. It's also important to check in on each other's motivation and progress. As the leader, set the example by asking people how they are feeling. Where did they struggle with their motivation, and where did they thrive?

We know that this approach works because we used it during the financial crisis. When most financial services teams were doubling down on rules and processes, we helped thousands of people working in mortgage and home equity shops identify the problems they could solve, innovate, and adapt. Their motivation skyrocketed, and they outperformed the status quo by 200%, finding creative win-win solutions for the financial institutions they worked at and the customers who were in danger of losing their homes.

It is possible for teams to experiment and adapt. Make it your mission to achieve greater levels of growth and productivity as a remote team than as an in-person team. This is a challenge that can keep you energized and experimenting long into the future.

Lindsay McGregor is coauthor of the *New York Times* bestseller *Primed to Perform* and cofounder and CEO of Vega Factor, a technology and consulting firm dedicated to ending low-performing cultures. Previously, Lindsay was a consultant at McKinsey & Company, focused on large-scale transformations. Lindsay earned her bachelor's degree from Princeton University and her MBA from Harvard University.

Neel Doshi is coauthor of the *New York Times* bestseller *Primed to Perform* and cofounder of Vega Factor. Previously, Neel was a partner at McKinsey & Company, the CTO of Genesant Technologies, and Technology Director of Finance.com. Neel earned his bachelor's degree in engineering from MIT and his MBA from the Wharton School.

CHAPTER 23

Tips for Coaching Someone Virtually

by Ed Batista

Leaders are providing less explicit direction to their employees these days and relying more on coaching as a leadership tool, as organizations become flatter and more dependent on knowledge work. But many people also manage teams that span locations and time zones, which means they must do at least some of their coaching virtually.

While most of my coaching with clients and MBA students at Stanford is conducted face-to-face in the Bay Area, over the last decade I've worked with people across the U.S. and internationally, from Brazil to London to

Adapted from "Tips for Coaching Someone Remotely" on hbr.org, March 18, 2015 (product #H01XI4).

South Africa. Here are some guidelines for virtual coaching that I've found useful.

Don't Dictate the Medium

You may have a preference for phone or video, or your organization may rely on one more than the other. But for coaching conversations, it's important that both parties choose what's right for the situation, rather than have it dictated by you as the leader or by the organizational culture.

In my experience, both phone and video can work well for coaching. One isn't better than the other, but they are *different*, and it's important to get a sense of which medium will work best for each relationship (this may change from call to call). Video can provide helpful visual context, but it can also be a distraction, particularly if there's a poor internet connection. Try experimenting with both phone and video to see what works best with different employees.

Email can play a useful role in virtual coaching, but I recommend using it to augment phone or video conversations. I often email my clients and students follow-up questions and links to readings and other resources, but it's much less useful for in-the-moment coaching. Text and chat provide a sense of immediate connection, but it's difficult to use them to convey anything more complex than basic information.

Location Still Matters

The physical setting can have a significant impact on the success of a coaching conversation. When I'm coaching clients and students in person, we meet in a place that will allow for privacy and minimal distractions. This can take many forms, from a reserved conference room to a long walk around the placid Stanford campus.

Because it's far more difficult to pick up interpersonal cues when working virtually, it's even more important to ensure that both you and the other person are in a private, comfortable space where you won't be interrupted.

Focus, Focus, Focus

Effective coaching in any setting requires focused attention on the other person. That can be tough when we're coaching virtually, because of the pervasiveness of multi-tasking. A virtual coaching conversation is a special kind of interaction—very different from a typical conference call or online meeting, where we can often just partly tune in and still get the gist. When we're coaching, the most important details are easy to miss. If we allow ourselves to become distracted, we'll be less likely to notice things like a subtle change in someone's facial expression or tone of voice, or an unusual turn of phrase that may signify something more. We may also fail to monitor our own emotional responses and instincts, which are vital sources of data. Even worse, others can sense when our attention wanders, leaving them reluctant to discuss truly important issues.

Get the Right Equipment

Investing in better technical gear can dramatically improve the virtual coaching experience. One of the clients I work with via video is a CEO who leads a virtual financial services firm. Almost all of his employees are spread out across the country, and they do most of their collaboration online. His home office is equipped with high-quality webcams, monitors, and microphones that give him a vivid virtual presence. Our video coaching sessions aren't quite as high-definition as real life, but they're close.

Even small investments in equipment can go a long way. I worked with a CEO who had a slight speech impediment that made it difficult for me to understand him over the phone. We had no problems communicating when we met in person, but most of our work was going to be virtual, so I bought the kind of immersive headset that's used by video gamers, which allowed me to understand him perfectly. I also have an external microphone and speakers so that when I'm working with clients via video I don't have to rely on my laptop components.

Manage the Time

In most meetings, including phone calls and videoconferences, the discussion goes right up until the end of the allotted time, at which point we rapidly conclude and move on to the next meeting. This is another way in which coaching conversations are different: It's part of your job, as the coach, to track time during the conversation—I usually set a timer to minimize distractions—and stop at a point you've agreed on in advance.

It's hard to tell where coaching conversations will end up. They tend to be more wide-ranging than typical meetings, which makes them more meaningful and valuable. But this also means you'll want to leave some time between the end of the session and the next event on the calendar. This enables both you and the person you're coaching to reflect on the conversation and deepen the learning. Coaching conversations can also bring up strong emotions, and it's essential to leave time to process those emotions. Even a few minutes can make a substantial difference, helping both you and the person you're coaching get the most out of the experience.

Ed Batista is an executive coach and a lecturer at the Stanford Graduate School of Business. He writes regularly on issues related to coaching and professional development at edbatista.com, contributed to the *HBR Guide to Coaching Employees*, and is currently writing a book on self-coaching for HBR Press.

CHAPTER 24

How to Manage a Remote Employee Who's Struggling to Perform

by Ron Carucci

"You need to make Anil do his job!"

My client—let's call her Robin—received this text from her sales manager during their virtual leadership meeting. Like many managers today, Robin is feeling the pressure of remotely running a $1.5 billion division of a food manufacturer.

Anil, her customer operations manager, was a strong performer back in the office. Remote work, however,

Adapted from "How to Manage an Employee Who's Struggling to Perform Remotely" on hbr.org, May 19, 2020 (product #H05M6T).

has not been kind to him. Though he claimed to have his tasks under control, with three children under 10 and a wife who also works, things were falling through the cracks. Salespeople had begun to receive complaints from desperate restaurant customers. Orders were arriving incorrectly and late. Since their businesses depend on every order to survive, these mistakes posed a serious threat.

Despite being an empathetic and skilled leader, Robin was struggling to hold Anil accountable. Difficult conversations are her Achilles' heel, and she's not alone. One study shows that 18% of top executives say holding others accountable is their greatest weakness. Add to that the challenge of giving feedback virtually, and you've got quite an obstacle to overcome.

At the same time, an employee who isn't keeping up while working remotely is a problem that cannot be ignored. In fact, poor performance consumes up to 17% of a leader's job[1] (equivalent to roughly one day a week), and in an uncertain economy, its financial costs are intensified.

So how can leaders like Robin confront team members who are struggling to successfully work remotely while also remaining sensitive to those employees' difficulties? It requires a broader approach and different skills than many leaders are used to. But there are several ways to learn them:

Expand Your Diagnostic Lens

With many unfamiliar variables introduced by Covid-19, getting to the bottom of a new performance problem is more complicated. Prior to the pandemic, most leaders might have reflexively zeroed in on the underperformer as the primary unit of analysis and presumed the problem was the result of insufficient skills, lack of initiative, inadequate commitment, or a poor attitude.

While these often play some role in underperformance, they rarely account for all of it. That's why focusing on the underperformance versus the *underperformer* leads to better problem-solving. This is especially true today, when myriad new factors could be contributing to the issue.

Before confronting your underperformer, use these questions to help you figure out what those factors may be:

What's different?

When you're dealing with someone who has just recently started to underperform, begin by identifying new variables that could be interfering with their work. Have there been recent organizational shifts? Difficulties in their personal life? For many, working from home presents several technical and self-management challenges. Isolating which factors may be causing legitimate obstacles to your employee's job will require you to have sensitive and persistent conversations with them. In the case of Robin, she assumed that Anil's demanding home life was a large factor. Feeling bad for him, she refrained from addressing the issue. As it turns out, her hesitance kept the real causes concealed.

What's worse?

Working virtually, as many of us are or have, will undoubtedly amplify weak areas of your organization:

Clunky processes may feel more cumbersome; getting information in a culture of secrecy may now feel impossible; work-arounds people have adopted to cope with outmoded technologies will likely break down. But leaders must be able to identify which broader organizational performance concerns may be contributing to an employee's performance issue. Sometimes you may not know until you have the conversation, but it's important to consider all the factors before a confrontation. You want your employee to trust that you've thought through the situation and considered it from their view. They will be less likely to use those broader issues as an excuse.

What's fact, and what's emotion?

Anxiety, anger, and fear can lead to blame, defensiveness, and irrationality, which worsen when we're isolated. As such, it's even more critical to separate emotion from fact in these situations. Leaders experiencing frustration around an underperformer will need to acknowledge the presence of these emotions, and honor them, before they are able to set them aside. Once you do, you will be more equipped to discuss what is factually true. In Robin's case, the team's and customers' anger amplified her and Anil's guilt, clouding everyone's judgment about how to identify and solve the real problem.

What's mine, and what's theirs?

Healthy accountability starts with a leader acknowledging that they may play a role in someone's underperformance. Have you been clear about what you expect from your newly remote team? Have you provided needed resources, coaching, and feedback? Is a gap in your leadership contributing to the problem? Robin's misassumption about Anil's stressful home life became the perfect excuse to justify not addressing him. But this contributed to the problem. Anil's failure to ask for help, offer creative solutions, and set expectations about his new normal were his contributions to the problem.

Show Empathy Without Lowering the Bar

"Whom do I throw under the bus?" Robin asked me. "My customers, who need my products to survive, or one of my top leaders, who is up against tough constraints with a family to care for?" Her unmanaged anxiety and confrontation avoidance backed her into a false-binary corner, leading her to ask the wrong question. What she needed to ask was, "How do I help my key leader succeed?" Ultimately, she was confusing empathy with lowered expectations. Her fear of making Anil "feel bad" wasn't compassion, it was cowardice.

You can demonstrate your care for an employee's struggles by both acknowledging their hardship *and* redoubling efforts to help them succeed. The best way to have these conversations virtually is through a video call, so you can read one another's tone and expressions. When you start the discussion, remember that this behavior is new for your employee too, and they are likely already feeling bad for struggling. "Check in" before you "check on" as a rule. Ask how they are doing in order to gauge their well-being. Then, clarify that your goal for the conversation is to help resolve the problem at hand.

To begin, use probing questions like, "Why do you feel this is happening?" Listen carefully to how they describe the situation. If they deny there is a problem, you may have mismatched expectations. If they point fingers, make repeated excuses, or refuse to take responsibility, you may have someone in the wrong role.

When Robin finally confronted Anil, she discovered that the fulfillment process at her company was the real problem. Their data systems were still tied together by laborious manual processes, including spreadsheets, heroics, and hallway handoffs. To avoid catastrophes in the office, Anil and his team routinely ran between buildings with key information. Now, as a remote worker, "running between buildings" had become endless texts, instant messages, and emails. Anil couldn't keep up.

Through their conversation, Robin realized that Anil shouldn't be off the hook from delivering the same level of results he did before. But the path to those results might need to shift, and it was her job, as the leader, to help Anil discover that path.

Engage the Underperformer in Problem-Solving

In my experience, performance shortfalls, especially sudden ones, are best resolved by asking the person in question to be responsible for solving the problem. Once you've identified the issue, ask, "What would you change if you could?" or "What can we all learn from this?" to open their imagination and signal that you trust their ability to improve.

Resist telling them *what* to do or being overly pro-scriptive about *how* to do it. You don't want to dilute their ownership and commitment. Remember that working in isolation can make people more anxious about their mistakes, and this is a person who is used to seeing success. Reassuring your employee that you are OK with missteps as long as they are corrected and learned from will help empower them to solve the problem on their own. At the same time, you should remain available to provide guidance when needed. This may require insti-tuting more-frequent check-ins to compensate for the changing conditions.

To redirect her conversation with Anil, Robin asked, "What can we do right now to help you? How can our whole team help make sure every order is on time and accurate?" This gave Anil permission to ask for help without deepening his shame. It also opened the door to creative interim solutions. "I know these are tough days, and I know we can do better," she said. "I need you to come back to me with a plan you are confident will get all orders out the door on time and accurately."

Anil took less than a day to build a plan and get his peers on board.

Strengthen Team Accountability

There a few things you can do to avoid this issue from reoccurring in the future. One of them is making sure that your team members realize their collective success belongs to one another—not just to you, the boss. Other-wise, you'll end up playing air traffic control for every result the team delivers, and you will spend more time managing what falls through the cracks than helping them achieve greater performance.

The toughest question I asked Robin was, "Why do you suppose your sales manager felt it was appropriate to send that text to you, instead of something more generative to Anil like, 'Anil, we can see you are struggling. How can we help?'" Robin was stumped. I told her this interaction could be exposing another problem: excessive reliance on her for the team's performance. I suggested that Robin go back to her sales manager and ask what it would have taken for him to reach out directly to Anil.

To avoid the situation Robin found herself in, there is one exercise you can use to strengthen your team's sense of shared accountability. In your next meeting, ask every person to identify how they rely on each of their fellow team members. Then compare answers. There should be explicit commitments they each make to one another, in which you remain uninvolved.

Remember, your biggest contribution to those you lead is helping them be, and contribute, their best. When they fall short, your greatest show of compassion is to help them figure out whatever it takes to get back on track. In some cases, it may be more compassionate to loosen expectations, as long as you make that decision *with* people and not *for* them.

Ron Carucci is cofounder and managing partner at Navalent, working with CEOs and executives to pursue transformational change for their organizations, leaders, and industries. He is the best-selling author of eight books, including *Rising to Power*. Connect with him on Twitter: @RonCarucci.

NOTE

1. Terri Williams, "Don't Let Low Performers Destroy Your Company," *The Economist*, https://execed.economist.com/blog/career-hacks/dont-let-low-performers-destroy-your-company.

Solving Problems on a Remote Team

CHAPTER 25

How to Collaborate Effectively If Your Team Is Remote

by Erica Dhawan and Tomas Chamorro-Premuzic

Remote communication isn't always easy. Do you recognize yourself in any of these examples?

At 10 p.m., a corporate lawyer gets a text from a colleague and wonders (not for the first time) if there's a protocol about work-related texts after a certain hour.

After a long and liquid client dinner, an advertising executive opens an email from his boss reminding him to

---

Adapted from content posted on hbr.org, February 27, 2018 (product #H046TS).

submit his expenses on time. Annoyed by this microman-agement, he immediately responds with his uncensored thoughts.

On the weekly team conference call, a remote team member is confused about whether her colleague is re-ally "on mute" when she delays a response to a question or if she's just not paying attention and is using this as an excuse.

When it's possible to be set off by a phone's mute but-ton, it's safe to say that we're living in challenging times. The digital era has ushered in a revolution in commu-nication that's equivalent to the one surrounding the invention of the printing press. It's changing how we speak—often in bullet points. And it's affecting what we hear, as the jumble of information coming at us can lead to frequent misunderstandings and confusion.

People who work on remote teams face these chal-lenges consistently—and as more and more of us are in-cluded in that group, we'll need a new range of behaviors and skills.

Why do remote teams demand new collaboration skills? What's missing from our texts, emails, confer-ence calls, and other digital communications? Body lan-guage. Even when we're colocated, the tone of a text or the formality of an email is left wide open to interpreta-tion, to the point that even our closest friends get con-fused. These misinterpretations create an anxiety that can become costly, affecting morale, engagement, pro-ductivity, and innovation.

Remote communication can distort the normal pace of our conversations. The delay between our messages can often postpone or hide emotional reactions to our comments. How many times have you written an email and, immediately after hitting send, felt concerned about how it would land? Would your boss see your late-night email and consider it to be an intrusion on her private time? Would she tell you if it was? While we may have become used to these types of asynchronous interactions, they can still conflict with our normal rules for social interaction. Lacking an immediate response, we can become distracted, second-guess ourselves, or even grow frustrated with our teams.

To perform at the highest levels, remote teams have to find new and better ways to operate. When they communicate well and leverage their strengths, remote teams can actually gain an advantage over colocated teams. Here are some best practices to master:

Don't conflate brief communications and clear communications

In our efforts to be efficient, we sometimes use fewer words to communicate. But such brevity can mean that the rest of the team wastes time trying to interpret your messages. (And then misinterprets them anyway.) Don't assume that others understand your cues and shorthand. Spend the time to communicate with the intention of being ultraclear, no matter the medium. Indeed, you can never be *too* clear, but it is too easy to be less clear than you should be.

Don't bombard your team with messages

Do you follow up on a task by email, text, *and* phone? Do you tend to ask people if they got your previous message? Abusing those access points can be a form of digital dominance, a relentless and uncomfortable form of harassment. The medium you choose creates different demands on the time of the receiver. Using all of them for the same message is ineffective (as well as annoying). Choose your digital volume wisely.

Establish communication norms

Remote teams need to create new norms that establish clarity in communication. Companies such as Merck have created acronyms for their digital communications like "Four Hour Response (4HR)" and "No Need to Respond (NNTR)" that bring predictability and certainty to virtual conversations. Individual teams can also establish their own norms—e.g., to use (or not use) Slack, Google Docs, or WhatsApp groups. And norms can also exist on an individual level, such as people's preferred response time, writing style, and tone. For example, some individuals prefer short and quick messages, while others favor lengthy and detailed responses; people also differ in their preference and tolerance for humor and informality.

While we often tend to regard human predictability as a defect, few qualities are more sought-after at work, especially in virtual collaborations. We are all unique, but our consistent behaviors help others predict what we do and in turn help them to understand us—and we all benefit from being understood. You can make that easier for others by establishing a clear personal etiquette and sticking to it consistently.

See the hidden opportunities in written communications

Being behind a screen can create new opportunities for certain team members, making space for those who might be less inclined to speak out in groups. Text-based communication places less importance on interpersonal skills and physical appearance, offering an effective way to share power and decision making. Research shows that introverted individuals are less inhibited in online versus offline interactions.[1] However, you need to watch out for *virtual unconscious bias*, where punctuation, grammar, and word choice might reveal prejudiced attitudes toward certain groups.

And the absence of body language doesn't necessarily mean that we're not giving away more than we intend to when we communicate remotely. There's still a great deal of metacommunication and virtual leakage that happens in digital environments, and it only takes paying attention to read between the lines. For example, the use of exclamation marks or a negative emoji after referring to someone's gender, nationality, or religion is as powerful a marker of disapproval as a disgusted face.

Create intentional space for celebration

Old-school birthday cakes are still important for remote teams. Creating virtual spaces and rituals for celebrations and socializing can strengthen relationships and lay the foundation for future collaboration. Find ways to shorten the affinity distance. One company we worked with celebrated new talent by creating a personal emoji for each employee who had been there for six months. You can find your own unique way to create team spaces for social connection. How you do it is less important than whether you do.

As more and more of our interactions happen digitally, we will continue to experience new forms of miscommunication and misunderstanding. The solution will not come from new technologies (although, no doubt, developers will keep trying to bridge that gap). Instead, the solution is in understanding the new rules of engagement—in building a communication skill set that reflects the demands of our digitally driven age.

Erica Dhawan is the author of the forthcoming book *Digital Body Language*. She's also a keynote speaker and the CEO of Cotential, a global training firm that delivers 21st-century collaboration skills in a digital-first marketplace. Follow her on Twitter: @edhawan.

Tomas Chamorro-Premuzic is the Chief Talent Scientist at ManpowerGroup, a professor of business psychology at University College London and at Columbia University, and an associate at Harvard's Entrepreneurial Finance Lab. He is the author of *Why Do So Many Incompetent Men Become Leaders? (and How to Fix It)*, upon which his TEDx talk was based. Find him at www.drtomas.com or on Twitter: @drtcp.

NOTE

1. Jin K. Hammick and Moon J. Lee, "Do Shy People Feel Less Communication Apprehension Online? The Effects of Virtual Reality on the Relationship Between Personality Characteristics and Communication Outcomes," *Computers in Human Behavior* 33 (April 2014): 302–310, https://www.sciencedirect.com/science/article/pii/S0747563213000496.

CHAPTER 26

Managing a Team Across 5 Time Zones

by Donna Flynn

It's 5:00 p.m. at my house in Nederland, Colorado, and I remember that I have a 6:00–7:30 p.m. team meeting. I need to plan the family dinner around it. I head to the kitchen to prep chicken and vegetables, timing them so they will roast and rest during my meeting and we can sit down to eat as soon as I am done. In Grand Rapids, several team members will join the meeting at 8:00 p.m., after their dinners and evening plans. In Hong Kong, it will be 8:00 a.m. and Elise and Yushi will either be at the

---

Adapted from content posted on hbr.org, June 17, 2014 (product #H00V3S).

studio or still at home, since the train commute can take a while. In San Francisco, Meike will likely call in from the Coalesse Studio. The meeting today is "no Paris" since it is 2:00 a.m. there and Beatriz will be sleeping.

At Steelcase, we all understand that the rhythm of a global team is not a perfect 9-to-5 melody. But understanding something can be very different from living it. My team has grown increasingly distributed across multiple time zones and regions of the world over the last couple of years, and we have learned, through experience and experimentation, a few ways to leverage the value of a global team while also minimizing the pain and disruption it can create for us as individuals. Since this is a shared experience for many multinational teams, I thought I would share five good global-team practices we've adopted.

Share the Burden of 24-7 Across the Team

We will never be able to change our human circadian rhythms, even though some of us may be early birds and others night owls. Time separation on a global team presents one of the biggest physical, cognitive, and emotional challenges. Despite all our "understanding" of being a global team, we used to always privilege Grand Rapids, Michigan (U.S. Eastern Time), in our meeting schedule and make our Asia team members stay up late. We changed the cadence to privilege different time zones once per month by rotating meeting times. Every month, each team member now has one evening, one midday, and one early-morning meeting, and misses one meeting that falls in the middle of their night. No team member is expected to attend a team meeting between 10 p.m. and 7 a.m.

Schedule Consistent Meetings

Serendipitous encounters with colleagues around the world are still limited with our current technologies. We have learned that having consistent meetings where people can connect in both formal and informal ways is critical for fostering team cohesion. Our team has weekly meetings to provide this structure—and we make them long enough to allow for technology connection hiccups, formal sharing of project work, and some time for catching up on vacations, travel experiences, or life-stage celebrations like engagements or new babies. We are also prototyping a global "social hour" where we are all invited to bring coffee, lunch, or a cocktail—depending on where you are and what time it is—and hang out together on videoconference. Every team needs to think about what may be best for them, but you'll want more of these checkpoints than you would need for a fully colocated team.

Use as Many Collaboration Tools as You Need

The tools available to distributed teams today aren't perfect. There is no one technology that does everything we need, so we use many of them for different purposes—including Google Drive, Dropbox, Spark, and MURAL. We have fully adopted MURAL (a digital, highly visual, sticky-note canvas) as a team in the last year, and it has dramatically improved our team's collaboration.

Video conferencing applications have come a long way and are continuously improving, but there are still challenges. Though we have high-resolution tele-presence in our offices, inevitably some team members joining from home can't connect. We have cycled through several desktop video platforms in the last few years, and are constantly learning new ones, and they all have their individual quirks. We've found that it takes a lot of patience and flexibility to use these tools effectively, as well as adaptability in swapping out tools in the moment as needed—such as dropping an unstable video connection and switching to conference call because the bandwidth in Hong Kong is experiencing latency.

Pay Extra Attention to Remote Colleagues

At Steelcase, we talk a lot about the concept of "presence disparity." In meetings that bring people together via different communication channels, individual "presences" don't necessarily have the same weight in the conversation. For example, people in the same room are more likely to talk to each other and forget about the person on the video screen and the person on the speakerphone. Likewise, it's easier to enter the conversation as a distributed participant on video than from the phone, because your visual presence makes it easier to get people's attention.

We are constantly looking for new ways to solve for this reality of modern communications at Steelcase—and yet too often our own teams succumb to its allure by privileging those who are physically present over those who are joining from afar. The most powerful tool for this is *awareness*—remember the value that your colleagues around the world bring to the table and honor them with consistent inclusion in the conversation. Practice eye contact with people on video, gently pause a passionate conversation in the room and ask the remote participants to chime in, or experiment with equalizing presence by having everyone call into the video conference or conference call individually.

Bring the Team Together to Foster Cohesion

No tool can replace being together in the same room. I bring my globally dispersed team together twice a year for workshops, which has proven invaluable for renewing personal ties, building trust, and having unmediated and embodied experiences together. I have three rules for these workshops: We should build something together, we should learn something together, and we should have plenty of informal social time. I also use these times for us to engage in team strategic discussions or decision making, since it's much more effective to reach alignment around complex issues when we are in the same room.

For instance, one year, we all gathered in Paris for our spring workshop. We finalized our team goal for the coming fiscal year and developed our integrated team plan with clear alignment to our corporate strategy and fiscal-year priorities (we built something together). We spent an afternoon envisioning our team future through an experimental theater exercise developed at Otto Scharmer's Presencing Institute at MIT and another afternoon visiting a museum (we learned together). Finally, we ate a lot of good French food and tasted some local wines, too (we had informal social time). The travel costs for these two weeks every year spurs our team's performance for the other 50 weeks. A smart travel budget is a necessary component for a high-performing, globally integrated team.

If you're unable to travel, you can still bring the team together regularly, even in a virtual way. Consider a remote off-site or other virtual activities through which your team can work together and bond over shared experiences. (For more on virtual off-sites, flip back to chapter 17.)

All of these different approaches add up to increasing our team's empathy for one another. This compassion fuels trust, engagement, and collaboration—and drives our business forward.

Donna Flynn is vice president, global talent at Steelcase.

CHAPTER 27

How to Raise Sensitive Issues with Your Remote Team

by Joseph Grenny

Hassan jammed a pencil eraser into his palm over and over in frustration.

He was 80 minutes into a virtual meeting with counterparts from five other countries. A financial downturn had cut their revenue outlook dramatically. Those on the call had been tasked with taking 15% out of their cost structure, to help the company survive the impending

---

Adapted from "How to Raise Sensitive Issues During a Virtual Meeting" on hbr.org, March 14, 2017 (product #H03IFN).

revenue famine. On last month's videoconference, all six of them had committed to terminating consulting contracts as one immediate measure. But a few days later Hassan learned that his Indonesian colleague, who was in the virtual meeting, had violated the commitment by extending a three-year engagement on a pet project. Hassan knew that at least three other colleagues on the call were aware of the broken commitment. But no one was saying anything.

In fact, the meeting leader said, "Looks like we've covered everything on the agenda. Any other issues anyone wants to address?"

Three decades of researching human behavior has taught me that you can generally measure the health of a team, relationship, or even an entire organization by measuring the average lag time between identifying problems and discussing them. The longer issues go unaddressed, the higher the price you pay in trust, engagement, decision making, productivity, quality, safety, diversity—you name it.

And yet my company's research shows that, in typical organizations, 72% of people fail to speak up when a peer doesn't pull their weight and 57% let peers slide when they've skirted important workplace processes.[1] People bite their tongue for weeks, months, and sometimes forever. Meanwhile, bad decisions get made, customers are hurt, bad behavior goes unchecked, and employee cynicism festers.

For example, we found that virtual teammates are 2.5 times more likely to perceive mistrust, incompetence, broken commitments, and bad decision making with distant colleagues than those who are colocated. Worse, they report taking 5 to 10 times longer to address their concerns.

This growing malady will increasingly drag organizational performance down unless leaders develop competence and norms in their organizations to address even the most sensitive issues quickly and directly—sometimes even in the middle of a virtual meeting.

The reason so few of us speak up about sensitive issues is that we are wired for mistrust. More humans survived over the millennia by assuming ill intent on the part of others than the opposite. As a result, we have a conservative bias: When in doubt, play it safe. Hide in a bush. Pick up a rock. Keep silent.

To shrink the lag time between the emergence and the addressing of concerns in virtual teams, you need to create *safety*. When people feel safe, they open up. When they don't, they shut down. People only feel safe enough to venture into dicey dialogue when those around them generate sufficient positive evidence of their intentions and respect.

Here's how to create candor when it matters most.

Demonstrate trustworthiness

The reason virtual teams are breeding grounds of mistrust is that a lack of physical contact starves us of data about where we stand in the group. When you're on a virtual team, you should assume that you'll need to address something difficult as the project progresses—and proactively generate evidence of your trustworthiness in advance of the concerns. Even the smallest of gestures can fill the void of information that distance creates. Be generous with information. Be the first to offer help. Send a congratulatory email when others succeed. A little kindness goes a long way in helping others interpret your intentions differently when inevitable stresses arise.

Ask for permission

When it comes time to raise an issue in a virtual meeting, ask for permission. For example, Hassan could begin with, "Yes, I've got an issue to address. It's pretty sensitive but pretty important. May I proceed?" Asking for permission may seem perfunctory, but it is psychologically significant. Nothing violates safety like surprise. Giving people an opportunity to opt out gives them a feeling of control. Signal your positive intentions and respect by giving advance warning. If you can deliver this request in a calm, open manner, your tone of voice will reinforce your words.

Share what you don't want

When you're worried about others misunderstanding your intentions, inoculate them against their misinterpretation by calling it out. For example, Hassan could say, "Hinata, I've got a rumor I want to address that pertains to you. I don't want to put you on the spot or disrespect you in any way. But I also want to be loyal to the mission we've been given, and I believe you do, too. This is an integrity issue to me—that is where I'm coming from."

Tell the story slowly, facts first

Lay out the factual basis for your concerns. Strip out any accusatory language. Pause to confirm your facts as you go. Tone of voice is everything. Don't accuse or attack; simply state what you think is correct. For example, say, "At our last meeting, we agreed to cancel consulting contracts. Was that your understanding, Hinata? As I contacted our supply chain consultant to cancel our Malaysia engagement, he informed me that the day before, you had not canceled the contract with him but rather had extended it for three years."

Share tentative conclusion and invite dialogue

Next, share what you've concluded from these facts, but do so in a way that leaves room for discussion. "That seems to contradict our agreement. Am I missing something here? Did you do this, or is there more to the story?"

Generate follow-up evidence of your goodwill

Once the issue is addressed and settled, reconfirm your intentions and respect through your subsequent behavior. As appropriate, send an email to reconfirm any assurances you gave—without apologizing for any grievances you may have expressed.

These suggestions don't guarantee that a virtual conversation will go well, but they significantly increase the likelihood. And take heart, because even if a first attempt is rocky, you can generate more safety with how you act following the conversation. The only way to help a virtual team develop the norm of holding crucial conversations promptly is to *hold them*, even if they don't go well at first.

In the end, Hassan said nothing. Instead, he used Hinata's apparent transgression as an excuse to continue his work with his own consultants. This, of course, was not good for the team or the company. Trouble in virtual teams almost always begins when members choose to act out rather than talk out their concerns.

———————————

Joseph Grenny is a four-time *New York Times*–best-selling author, keynote speaker, and leading social scientist for business performance. His work has been translated into 28 languages, is available in 36 countries, and has generated results for 300 of the *Fortune* 500. He is the cofounder of VitalSmarts, an innovator in corporate training and leadership development.

NOTE

1. VitalSmarts, "Costly Conversations: Why the Way Employees Communicate Will Make or Break Your Bottom Line," December 6, 2016, https://www.vitalsmarts.com/press/2016/12/costly-conversa tions-why-the-way-employees-communicate-will-make-or-break -your-bottom-line/.

CHAPTER 28

Ideas for Helping Remote Colleagues Bond

by Kuty Shalev

Research consistently shows that remote employees tend to feel excluded from the company culture. They report feeling as if they are not treated equally and often fear that their colleagues are working against them. When a problem arises, nearly half of remote workers let it fester for weeks or more.

To improve workplace integration, my company experimented with several ways to bring our distributed workers together, including virtual coffees, book clubs,

---

Adapted from content posted on hbr.org, February 6, 2019 (product #H04RXB).

and executive-led webinars focused on values. Some of these efforts revved up the team temporarily, but they didn't solve the culture problems that are inherent to having a large remote workforce.

We realized that we needed to create a "beyond remote" workforce by coming together and creating an environment of bona fide cohesion and trust through meaningful relationships and conversations. Of all the methods we tried to bring scattered workers together, here are the two strategies that brought us the most success in terms of increasing engagement:

Generate Structured Conversations Around Shared Content

We set out to generate deeper conversations among co-workers through virtual meetings structured loosely like a book club but with a wider variety of content and platforms. For example, we had everybody watch the same TED talk, read the same book or article, or take the same online learning course. Then, we met via videoconference and asked everybody to share a reaction, with one person speaking and then choosing the next contributor to speak for about the same length of time. This selection process had the additional benefit of showing where social bonds are strongly developed or where they might need further development.

We found success in encouraging discussion and openness by starting with icebreaker questions as simple as "How did you take your coffee this morning?" If two people use oat milk, they might infer that they both value health, promoting further sharing and bonding. If we discuss an article's advice and ask, "Have you used these skills in your personal life?" we hear stories that reveal much more of the whole person and provide a greater glimpse into that person's character. Gathering this kind of direct knowledge about coworkers creates the kind of trust that's especially important in global teams.

Use Online Games to Help Build Trust

While this may sound unconventional, playing a video game—one chosen for its ability to force collaboration and to place the team in scenarios that are destined to fail—helps to build trust and reveal how the team will handle negative pressures. In her book, *Learning to Learn and the Navigation of Moods*, Gloria Flores discusses how the negative emotions that crop up when learning something new can block skill development. She stresses the importance of tools and prompts to help us push through. The gaming framework does just that: It allows team members to work through and even utilize the negative emotions that can arise during the learning process.

Deliberately choose a game that forces as many of your team members as possible to get out of their comfort zones. It's essential to create the equivalent amount of stress and the possibility of failure that exist at work. Imagine that the team is trying to get into a dungeon but is failing, and I'm yelling, "Your cannon wasn't in the right spot, and we're not coordinating. If you would only listen to me, maybe we'd get there!" Suddenly, that's an interesting conversation point: You think you're always right? Are you coordinating well? Are you giving good instructions and requests? Are people responding to you? Failures, and people's reactions to them, inspire much better conversations, as the team dynamics involved in game challenges often mimic the dynamics of work challenges.

Initially, we tried multiplayer games that included a mission for the team—think *Fortnite* or *League of Legends*—but our workers weren't failing enough. To heighten the situation, we switched to more complex games like *Factorio* that can stump even software developers who are more used to gaming. Adding this complexity provided a place where the team could safely learn from failures. In these heightened environments, people learned that they needed to speak up the moment they foresaw trouble, so they could renegotiate and form new goals or forge new paths. That alone has had a huge impact on interpersonal and work relationships within our own company.

While book clubs and gaming together may feel like they don't belong on company time, they have given our company a sense of cohesion and retention that had been missing. Our turnover had been significantly higher than the already high average in the software industry, and our retention rate has since improved. These tactics were a critical part of driving that number down. We've also seen a marked increase in progress on ongoing projects—even those that had been sitting on the back burner for a long time—and greater employee engagement. With these improvements, we've been able to set, and meet, new standards for ourselves. Coming together for nonwork activities enhanced our ability to coalesce around our common goals as a company.

———————

Kuty Shalev is the founder of Clevertech, a New York City–based firm that designs, develops, and deploys strategic software for businesses that want to transform themselves using the power of the web.

Index

Engage with HBR content the way you want, on any device.

With HBR's new subscription plans, you can access world-renowned **case studies** from Harvard Business School and receive **four free eBooks**. Download and customize prebuilt **slide decks and graphics** from our **Visual Library**. With HBR's archive, top 50 best-selling articles, and five new articles every day, HBR is more than just a magazine.

Subscribe Today
hbr.org/success

Smart advice and inspiration from a source you trust.

If you enjoyed this book and want more comprehensive guidance on essential professional skills, turn to the HBR Guides Boxed Set. Packed with the practical advice you need to succeed, this seven-volume collection provides smart answers to your most pressing work challenges, from writing more effective emails and delivering persuasive presentations to setting priorities and managing up and across.

Harvard Business Review Guides

Available in paperback or ebook format. Plus, find downloadable tools and templates to help you get started.

- Better Business Writing
- Building Your Business Case
- Buying a Small Business
- Coaching Employees
- Delivering Effective Feedback
- Finance Basics for Managers
- Getting the Mentoring You Need
- Getting the Right Work Done

- Leading Teams
- Making Every Meeting Matter
- Managing Stress at Work
- Managing Up and Across
- Negotiating
- Office Politics
- Persuasive Presentations
- Project Management

HBR.ORG/GUIDES

Buy for your team, clients, or event.
Visit hbr.org/bulksales for quantity discount rates.